ART AS
LANGUAGE

ART AS LANGUAGE

Access to Thoughts and Feelings through Stimulus Drawings

Rawley Silver, Ed.D.

USA	Publishing Office:	PSYCHOLOGY PRESS
		A member of the Taylor & Francis Group
		325 Chestnut Street
		Philadelphia, PA 19106
		Tel: (215) 625-8900
		Fax: (215) 625-2940
	Distribution Center:	PSYCHOLOGY PRESS
		A member of the Taylor & Francis Group
		7625 Empire Drive
		Florence, KY 41042
		Tel: 1-800-624-7064
		Fax: 1-800-248-4724
UK		PSYCHOLOGY PRESS
		A member of the Taylor & Francis Group
		27 Church Road
		Hove
		E. Sussex, BN3 2FA
		Tel.: +44 (0) 1273 207411
		Fax: +44 (0) 1273 205612

ART AS LANGUAGE: Access to Thoughts and Feelings through Stimulus Drawings

1 2 3 4 5 6 7 8 9 0

Printed by Edwards Brothers, Lillington, NC, 2001.
Cover design by Joe Dieter

A CIP catalog record for this book is available from the British Library.
   The paper in this publication meets the requirements of the ANSI Standard Z39.48-1984 (Permanence of Paper).

Library of Congress Cataloging-in-Publication Data

Silver, Rawley A.
   Art as language : access to thoughts and feelings through stimulus drawings /
   Rawley Silver.
       p. cm.
   Includes bibliographical references and index.
   ISBN 1-58391-051-4 (alk. paper)
       1. Children's drawings—Psychological aspects.   2. Children's art—Psychological
   aspects.   3. Art—Psychology.   4. Drawing, Psychology of.   5. Art therapy for children.
   6. Art therapy.   I. Title.
   BF723.D7 S57   2000
   155.4—dc21   00-046745

ISBN 1-58391-051-4

For Ed, Paul, and Jon

CONTENTS

LIST OF FIGURES

ACKNOWLEDGMENTS

The studies of reliability and validity could not have been carried out without the help of many art therapists and teachers who volunteered to administer the drawing tasks or score responses. Their assistance is gratefully acknowledged and appreciated. They include Doris Arrington, ATR-BC; Janice Bell, MA; Nancy Benson, MS; Allison Berman, ATR-BC; Andrea Bianco-Riete, ATR-BC; Eldora Boeve, MA; Sherry Carrigan, ATR-BC; Felix Carrion, ATR; Lin Carte, ATR-BC; Fran Chapman, MA; Linda Chilton, ATR; Bette Conley, ATR; Sylvia Corwin, MA; Georgette d'Amelio, MS; Peggy Dunn-Snow, PhD, ATR-BC; Joanne Ellison, ATR-BC; Patricia English, ATR; Betty Foster, MA; Cyrilla Foster, ATR; Phyllis Frame, ATR; Elizabeth Gayda, MA; Madeline Ginsberg, ATR-BC; Maryanne Hamilton, ATR-BC; Robin Hanes, ATR; Karen Hayes, MA; David Henley, ATR-BC; Ellen Horovitz, PhD, ATR-BC; Judith Itzler, ATR; Sara Jacobs Perkins, MA; Lynn Jamison, MS; Beth Kean, MA; Hope Larris-Carroll, ATR; Janeen Lewis, ATR; Madeline Masiero, ATR-BC; Jared Massanari, PhD; Eva Mayro, ATR; Carol McCarthy, ATR; Eileen McCormick Holzman, ATR; Maggie McCready, MA; Sally McKeever, MA; Sister Dorothy McLaughlin, ATR-BC; Kate McPhillips, MA, OTR; Christine Mercier-Ossorio, ATR; Yetta Miller, ATR; Constance Naitove, ATR; Ruth Obernbreit, ATR; JoAnne O'Brien, ATR; Bernice Osborn, MA; Norma Ott, MA; Carol Paiken, MA; Marcia Purdy, ATR; Lillian Resnick, ATR-BC; Michelle Rippey, ATR-BC; Kimberly Sue Roberts, ATR; Louise Sandburg, ATR; Sister Miriam Saumweber, ATR; Patricia Schachner, MS; Andrea Seepo, ATR; Joan Swanson, MA; Niru Terner, ATR; Sister Mary Tousley, ATR; Christine Turner, ATR-BC; Kristen Vilstrup, ATR-BC; Robert Vislosky, PhD, ATR; Mary Waterfield, ATR; Jules C. Weiss, ATR-BC; Simon Willoughby-Booth; Phyllis Wohlberg, ATR; and Shelley Zimmerman, ATR-BC.

I also express my gratitude to the psychologists who performed the statistical analyses. They (and the studies they analyzed) are: John L. Kleinhans, PhD (New York State Urban Education Project no. 147 232 101); Claire Lavin, PhD (National Institute of Education Project no. G 79

008); Beatrice J. Krauss, PhD (*Silver Drawing Test of Cognition and Emotion*); and Madeline Altabe, PhD (*Draw A Story: Screening for Depression*, and other studies published from 1992 to the present).

Finally, I thank the children and adults who created the drawings and stories reprinted here. Although I cannot reveal their names, I am deeply grateful for what they taught me.

FOREWORD

It is a great honor to be asked to write this Foreword for Rawley Silver's book, *Art as Language: Access to Emotions and Cognitive Skills through Drawings*. Many books discuss the application of artistic expressions, particularly drawings, to evaluate children and adults, but Dr. Silver brings a unique perspective to using drawings to assess developmental skills, imagination, thoughts, and feelings. In addition, she delivers an abundance of research data on these pages, proving the efficacy of art as a language and a means of communication for people of all ages.

For the last several decades, Dr. Silver has pioneered the premise that stimulus drawings (specific predrawn images) can be successfully used with children, adolescents, and adults to help us understand emotions and cognition. It has been long known that the visual arts provide a way of communicating thoughts and feelings too difficult to express with words, but few have undertaken the long-term research studies necessary to investigate and prove the effectiveness of drawings as a formal means of evaluation.

Early in her career, Dr. Silver began to work with children with hearing impairments and quickly discovered that these children often used art expression and imagination to convey fantasies of what they could not obtain in real life. This initial finding led her to a lifelong search to understand how images stimulated the imagination and served, in a sense, as another language.

In subsequent research, Dr. Silver also found that drawings provide an excellent way to evaluate developmental skills and emotional expression. Throughout this book, the author generously shares her expertise, her protocols and procedures, and decades of research. She offers the reader extensive information and studies (qualitative and quantitative) on the use of stimulus drawings with the following groups: children, adolescents, and adults; populations including those with emotional disturbance, learning disabilities, brain injuries, and hearing impairments; those with a history of sexual abuse and trauma; delinquent adolescents, sex offenders, and prisoners with psychiatric disorders; people with depression; and groups of varying age, gender, and culture.

I first encountered Dr. Silver's stimulus drawings while I was working as an art therapist and coordinator of children's services for a shelter for battered women and their children. I was struggling to understand and communicate with children who were witnesses to family violence and who often had been abused. Many of the children had difficulties in talking about their experiences, fearing repercussion for telling family secrets. Others, in addition to emotional trauma, had developmental problems that prevented them from expressing themselves with words. During the years I worked at that particular shelter I saw children who were learning disabled, children who had speech and hearing impairments, and children who were challenged by attention deficits and other difficulties.

I began using Dr. Silver's stimulus drawings as a way of not only evaluating the cognitive and creative skills of these children, but also as a way of reaching them. One experience with a six-year-old girl still remains vivid in my mind. The girl had just arrived at the shelter on the night before with her mother and had repeatedly witnessed the physical battering of her parent by an abusive boyfriend. Like many of the children I work with, she was fearful and anxious, apprehensive about her new surroundings, and mistrustful of the shelter staff, including me. And, like many children who have witnessed or been subjected to abuse, she was hesitant to talk about her experiences.

After letting her adjust to the art therapy room and explore the materials and play items, I asked her if she would like to look at some pictures with me and perhaps make a drawing about some of the pictures. She stared at me nervously until I laid out a small number of Silver's stimulus drawings in front of her on the art table. It was easy to see that the images intrigued her and she became engrossed in examining each simple line drawing until she stopped at one depicting a person sitting in a chair. I asked her at that point if she would like to use some of the crayons and a piece of drawing paper to make a picture using this image as her subject. She silently nodded and proceeded to recreate the image of the person in the center of the paper.

What was most striking about her drawing were the personal details she added to the image. She very carefully drew a frown on the person's face, brown hair and a dress like her own, and surrounded the figure with the outline of a house with a pitched roof, a schematic representation developmentally typical of a six-year-old child. She looked at me and said without any prompting, "This person is very, very sad to be in her house," as she pushed the drawing toward me. That picture and her simple description of it told me her story, succinctly and safely, and became the beginning of a productive and meaningful therapeutic relationship for both of us.

Although this experience occurred almost 20 years ago, Silver's work continues to be timely and relevant and has an important place in our understanding images, imagination, and creativity, and their role in emotions and cognition. What is most impressive about this book is the author's continuing research to understand what stimulus drawings can tell us about people, not only in emotional and cognitive areas, but also in age, gender, and cultural differences. Recently, researchers in Brazil and Australia have used Dr. Silver's stimulus drawings. I am sure that—with the publication of this book—researchers and clinicians in other parts of the world will soon be contributing new data on the use of stimulus drawings, extending our knowledge of how Dr. Silver's concepts can be used with an increasing variety of populations.

Engaging children, adolescents, and adults through imagery and imagination is one of few ways to reach many of the clients we see in therapy, in the clinic, or in the classroom. Creativity through drawing and storytelling helps to overcome the resistance to traditional therapy common in some populations. It also may be the only means of expression when words are difficult or unavailable, such as for those with disabilities or emotional disorders. Art can be another language, as Silver has demonstrated persuasively through her years of research, and it is unquestionably an effective means of evaluating and understanding people of all ages.

Cathy A. Malchiodi, ATR, LPAT, LPCC, REAT
Editor, Art Therapy: Journal of the American Art Therapy Association

STIMULUS DRAWING ASSESSMENTS

CHAPTER

Introduction

> The words or the language as they are written or spoken, do not seem to play any role in my mechanism of thought. The psychical entities which seem to serve as elements in thought are. . . in my case, of visual and muscular type. Conventional words or other signs have to be sought for laboriously only in a secondary stage. . .
>
> —Albert Einstein

This book considers how and why stimulus drawings can be used for access to fantasies, cognitive skills, and emotional needs. It attempts to link scientific observations with studio art experiences; to integrate objective knowledge with the subjective ways we perceive and represent the external world, and ourselves. It is also an attempt to pass along what I have learned about art as a language since I began working with language-impaired children in the 1960s, and about the abilities of typical and atypical children, adolescents, and adults.

I had studied painting and sculpture as a college student, then social work, and years later, returned for graduate education. I was working with deaf children who could neither read lips nor speak, and was trying to use visual art to stimulate their intellectual growth and ease their frustrations. Education in Art Therapy was not yet available, and if my dissertation had used the word "therapy," my doctorate would have been endangered. It seemed to me, however, that aesthetic and therapeutic goals did not need to conflict. I believed we could try to meet cognitive and emotional needs without neglecting art skills and aesthetic values.

This book is based on the premise that art can be a language parallel to the written word. Emotions and cognition can be evident in visual as well as verbal conventions. Although traditionally identified, assessed, and developed through words, emotions and cognition also can be identified, assessed, and developed through images. This introduction considers some views about nonverbal thinking, and expressing thoughts and feelings through drawings. It will also present an overview of how the book is organized.

☐ Nonverbal Thinking

The two lobes of the human brain seem to have different functions. As noted by Schlain (1998), the function of the right lobe is to perceive space, recognize images, and integrate feelings. The right lobe does not generate linguistic expression but is able to decipher nonverbal language, and generates metaphors, humor, intuitive insights, and feeling-states. We use the right lobe to read facial expressions, gestures, drawings, and emotional states, which are under less volitional control, and may even contradict what is said, like the hostess who urges her guest to stay, then yawns. We use the left lobe for speech, numbers, logical analysis, and abstract thinking, to describe, measure, and catalog objects, and to process information without images. These observations about brain functions are generally accepted, but views of the relationship between words and images are controversial.

Does verbal language *reflect* thought, or does it *produce* thought? I share the view that language follows, rather than precedes, logical thinking, and even though language expands and facilitates thought, high level thinking can and does proceed without it. As Jean Piaget (1970) observed, one-year-olds who have learned to pull a blanket to reach a toy on top, are capable of pulling the blanket to reach anything else, suggesting that logical thinking exists before the appearance of language. The linguist, Sinclair-de Zwart, originally believed that language produced thought, but after several experiments, concluded that language is structured by logic, not the other way round (1969).

According to Suzanne Langer (1957, 1958), art is a way of articulating thoughts and expressing experiences that cannot be put into words. The most universal form of expression is verbal, but speech is only one kind of symbolic process. Even with speech, "when we want to convey a new experience or a direct sensation, we turn to the imagery of art, to metaphor..." (Langer, 1957, p. 23).

It seemed to me that even though children (and adults) with language impairments were handicapped in representing their thoughts effectively, their capacity for symbolizing could remain intact, enabling them to use art symbols, like verbal symbols, to represent particular subjects or classes of subjects.

The painting of a man, for example, can represent the painter's father, authority figures in general, Man in the abstract, or all three, just as the word "man" can represent each or all of these ideas depending on the verbal context. If inarticulate children and adults were to express through drawings, the thoughts they cannot put into words, their drawings could provide useful clues to what they know and how they think and feel.

Recent findings by neurologists and others who study the brain can inform art therapists about the cognitive and emotional processes underlying the visual arts; we, in turn may be able to provide them with clues to where brain lesions are located in specific areas of the brain (as suggested by the responses to drawing tasks by a stroke patient, Gary, discussed in Chapter 6).

The neurologist, Antonio Damasio (1994), reports that human reason depends on several brain systems working in concert, and that feelings are a component and powerful influence on reasoning. Damasio was drawn to the topic of feelings as he struggled to understand the cognitive and neural machinery behind the defects of patients who had suffered brain injuries. The influence of feelings on cognition is immense, and contrary to some scientific opinion, feelings are just as cognitive as other precepts.

Frances Kaplan (2000) reviews the findings of neuroscience which indicate that graphic representation of images is a complex activity that involves areas of the brain intimately related to language, that art making can facilitate problem solving and other forms of creativity, stimulate feelings of pleasure and self-esteem, and provide opportunities for successful functioning by children and adults with cognitive impairments. She cites a cognitive scientist, Donald D. Hoffman (1998), who emphasizes the importance of visual intelligence by pointing out that the brain systems responsible for vision occupy nearly half of the cerebral cortex. Kaplan (2000) also cites neurologist R.M. Restak (1994) who notes that more brain neurons are devoted to vision than to any other of our senses, and art historian Ellen Dissanayake (1992) who observes that the arts have been consistently undervalued in recent times even though they involve a universal propensity of the human species that is a part of our biological and historical heritage.

☐ The Emotional Content of Drawings

Even without knowledge about the physiology of emotions, it is evident that emotions and cognition interact. Children who cannot keep up with their classmates academically tend to develop feelings of inadequacy; adults who lose the ability to speak often become depressed.

The visual arts provide an alternative channel for articulating feelings that are difficult to verbalize. They also provide access to fantasies because the nature of art experience is to invite subjectivity, as the nature of science is to invite objectivity. The paintings of Picasso or Rembrandt can be recognized at a glance.

Louis Tinnin (1990) has suggested that art making provides direct access to emotional memory, and that aesthetic sensibility, empathy, and emotion are rooted in unconscious mimicry. He describes unconscious mimicry as a capability of the nonverbal brain, similar to the cooperation seen in schools of fish, flocks of birds, and herds of animals. This capability is inaccessible to consciousness, and generally unknown to the dominant verbal hemisphere. Nonverbal therapies provide access to these mechanisms.

It would seem to follow that studio art experiences can stimulate sensitivity to expressions through visual art forms, and that training in both studio art and clinical psychology can enable art therapists to read subtle messages that may be inaccessible to their own conscious minds. This hypothesis has support in the differences found between art therapists and social workers who assessed self-images in drawings by delinquent adolescents (see the first study summarized in Chapter 9).

Responses to the stimulus drawing tasks suggest that both children and adults tend to identify with the subjects they choose and portray, using them to fulfill wishes vicariously, or express unacceptable feelings indirectly. Some respondents used written language freely while others had language impairments, but almost all were able to use drawing to convey thoughts and fantasies, or share feelings and perceptions.

Fulfilling Wishes Vicariously

Fantasies that represent wishes as fulfilled, actually do provide partial gratification, according to Brenner (1974) who noted that a thirsty dreamer, dreaming of quenching his thirst, goes on sleeping.

Some of my deaf students seemed to use their drawings as healing fantasies to obtain in imagination what they could not obtain in real life. Kenny, for example, age 14, had cerebral palsy and was notably small for his age, Figure 1-1 shows one of his many fantasies about riding a motorcycle, smoke and flags unfurling in his wake. Eileen liked to draw fantasies about romantic encounters. In one such drawing, a girl, swimming under a dark cloud, cries for help. A boy swims to her rescue. In a second drawing, Figure 1-2, the girl and boy are in a sailboat. "John" declares his love, she expresses gratitude, the sun smiles, the cloud is gone, and birds fly overhead. In a third drawing, Eileen also liked to fantasize about being rich (Fig. 1-3).

FIGURE 1-1. Kenneth and friend on motorcycle.

Expressing Anger and Fear Indirectly

Figure 1-4, began as a pencil drawing of a girl and boy. Then bleeding wounds were painted on their faces, suggesting anger toward them, and finally, stitches on their wounds suggesting the anger had been spent.

Figures 1-5, and 1-6 are fantasies about being murdered and committing suicide (suggesting anger directed toward self), topics that are discussed in other chapters.

☐ The Cognitive Content of Drawings

Some people expect competent drawings from educated adults and incompetent drawings from deaf children. Consider, though, two responses to one of the stimulus drawing tasks: Draw the way house would appear if moved from the mountain peak to a spot on the slope.

FIGURE 1-2. I Love You, Oh Thank You, by Eileen.

Figure 1-7 shows the response of an adult who participated in a workshop for teachers and mental health professionals. Figure 1-8 shows the response of a 13-year-old deaf child. The drawings suggest that the child, not the adult, was able to represent concepts of verticality.

These differences in ability, like the sophisticated drawings found on Paleolithic cave walls, should not be surprising. Although the sciences of ancient Greece, Egypt, and China, may be primitive when compared with contemporary sciences, their visual arts have not been excelled.

For some individuals, imagery seems to be the preferred mode of thinking. Witkin et al. (1962) observed that a preference for imagery is established early in life. Arnheim (1969) illustrated this preference with the different ways we respond to this question: What time will it be in half an hour if it is now 3:40 p.m.? One person uses arithmetic to find the answer, while another visualizes the face of a clock with its minute hand advanced from 8 to 2.

According to Sless (1981), the importance of vision in thinking has been obscured by the emphasis in our schools on literacy and numeracy. We tend to relegate vision to a peripheral role, separate from the mental activity of thought, but vision is not a sensory process. The "thinking eye" is evident in the embryo whose eyes develop before the brain, presumably

FIGURE 1-3. $90,000, I have more money, by Eileen.

FIGURE 1-4. Wounding, then suturing wounds.

Man
Kissl
A

FIGURE 1-5. Man Kissl A . . . .

FIGURE 1-6. Suicidal drawing.

to enable neural tissue to make use of visual information. As Sless points out, Watson visualized a helix in arriving at an understanding of the structure of DNA, and Kekule visualized the movement of atoms as a snake grabbing its tail.

Gardner (1993, p. 17) suggests that imagery represents spatial intelligence (one of seven kinds of intelligence), defined as the ability to form a mental model of the spatial world, and to maneuver and operate using

FIGURE 1-7. Response by an adult in a workshop for teachers and mental health professionals.

that model. Many individuals are gifted in spatial intelligence—surgeons, sailors, engineers, and scientists, as well as visual artists.

For children and adults who have difficulty putting thoughts into words, or understanding what is said, expression through visual art forms may be more than a matter of preference.

Some deaf children spontaneously make use of drawings to pin down, classify, and recall their experiences, as illustrated below.

Abstract Thinking

The thinking of deaf children is often characterized as concrete, but if a child who cannot talk about classifying, spontaneously depicted a category of events, it would seem to follow that he or she is able to represent abstract ideas. For example, Figure 1-9, a spontaneous drawing by Jane, age 11, shows children engaged in activities that are suitable for a particular location at a particular time of year. Her drawing seems to

FIGURE 1-8. Response by a 13-year-old with receptive and expressive language impairments.

represent a hypothetical event in which the various activities have elements in common—characteristics of an abstract idea.

Figure 1-10, I Love You Children, by Richard, age 12, seems to illustrate the observation that people say one thing but mean another. The words deny the symbol for poison, but being insincere, they reinforce the warning of the image—an abstract idea. Richard had exceptionally poor language skills for a deaf child his age, according to his classroom teacher, and he asked for help with spelling "children." If we had to depend on his verbal skills to judge his intelligence, we might have assumed that he was incapable of higher-level abstract reasoning.

Recall

We remember details more easily when we organize them into structured forms. It is easier, for example, to recall the words in a sentence than the same words at random on a list. Like a sentence, a drawing is a structured form.

In Rusty Nosed Boat, (Fig. 1-11), Ira drew the different shapes and sizes of whales, eels, dolphins, swordfish, and sharks, but did not label them,

FIGURE 1-9. Categorizing (games at the beach).

although he gave his boat its remarkable name. He asked to take his drawing home. When he returned with the picture, the fish had been identified by name, suggesting that this drawing had prompted him to learn the categories of fish that he represented.

Relationships Between Emotion and Cognition

Emotion and cognition seem to be separate but interacting mental functions, as Joseph Ledoux observed (1996). Emotions involve many more brain systems than thoughts, often allowing emotional arousal to dominate and control thinking. He also points out that both emotion and cognition seem to operate unconsciously, with only the outcome of emotional or cognitive processes entering awareness. He describes a brain-injured patient who could not remember her doctor when he left the room and returned a few minutes later. Nevertheless, she refused to shake his hand

FIGURE 1-10. The concept of insincerity.

again after he had pricked her with a tack concealed in his palm. Consciousness requires the capacity to relate several things at once—the way a stimulus looks, memories of past experiences with the stimulus (or a related stimulus), and awareness of the experiencing self.

Although Ledoux does not mention imagery or drawing, his observations illuminate the relationships between emotions and cognition in response to the stimulus drawing tasks.

☐ Organization

The following chapter presents an overview of three stimulus drawing assessments that the reader can use informally in working with children and adults. Formal testing calls for specific information in the test manuals.

Part II of this book presents qualitative studies of individuals who responded to the drawing tasks to indicate, how, why, and where the assessments can be useful. Respondents names throughout the book have been changed to protect their privacy. Additionally, respondents' spelling and grammar have not been corrected. Studies of emotionally disturbed children, adolescents, and adults are presented in Chapter 3, and studies

FIGURE 1-11. Ability to recall.

concerning learning disabled children and adolescents are in Chapter 4. Hearing impaired children and adolescents are discussed in Chapter 5 and brain-injured adolescents and adults are the focus of Chapter 6, and uses of humor in Chapter 7. Chapter 8 presents the developmental techniques that were used.

Part III reviews quantitative studies and the data collected from groups of typical and atypical respondents. Chapter 9 reviews studies of age and gender differences in responses by adolescents and adults in detention facilities, responses by children, adolescents, and adults with clinical or masked depression in schools or hospitals, by children with auditory or language impairments in special schools, and by learning disabled students in special schools, or in specialized programs in public schools.

Chapter 10 reviews the studies of age and gender differences among respondents with no known disabilities. These studies include attitudes toward self and others, toward the opposite sex, and toward food or eating and provide a look at senior adults, spatial intelligence, and cultural differences found among respondents living in the United States, Brazil, and Australia.

Stimulus Drawing Assessments

In the stimulus drawing approach, drawing takes the place of words as the principal channel for receiving and expressing ideas. Stimulus drawings (SDs) are used to elicit response drawings that are then scored on rating scales. The SDs consist of line drawings of people, animals, places, and things. Some are explicit; others are ambiguous to encourage associations with previous experiences.

The three SD assessments, and revised editions, were published between 1982 and 1996. They include *The Silver Drawing Test of Cognition and Emotion, Draw-A-Story, Screening for Depression,* and *Stimulus Drawings and Techniques in Therapy Development and Assessment.*

Different approaches to art therapy can specify what to draw or present unstructured drawing tasks (Allen, 1995; Gantt, 1990; Kramer, 1993; Lachman-Chapin, 1987; Levick, 1989; Malchiodi, 1998; Rubin, 1987; Ulman, 1987). The stimulus drawing approach offers a limited number of choices, based on the premise that structuring need not inhibit spontaneity if it can remain open-ended, and that setting limits can stimulate creativity and associations with previous experiences.

The three assessments present different sets of stimulus drawings from which to choose, but present virtually the same drawing from imagination task. In this task, respondents are asked to choose two or more stimulus drawings and imagine something happening between the subjects they choose; then draw what they have imagined.

They are encouraged to change the stimulus drawings and add their own subjects and ideas. Copying is discouraged, while expressiveness is encouraged. When drawings are finished, they are given titles or stories, and when feasible, are discussed so that meanings can be clarified.

The task is based on the observation that different individuals perceive the same stimulus drawings differently, and that responses tend to be both cognitive and emotional. Some respondents choose stimulus-drawings of animals or other subjects that represent themselves and others, in disguise, to distance themselves from painful experiences. Discussing a drawing from the subject's point of view also can provide distance from personal concerns.

In addition to the drawing from imagination task, the Silver Drawing Test presents two additional tasks: predicative drawing and drawing from observation, as will be discussed later on.

☐ How the Assessments Evolved

Originally, the stimulus drawings were attempts to communicate with children who had auditory or language disorders. I had volunteered to teach art in a school for deaf children after being temporarily deafened myself in an accident. Painting had been my vocation, and I wanted to share its pleasures with the children. Manual communication was forbidden in most schools for deaf children during the 1960s. Instead, the schools emphasized lip-reading and speech, and provided little or no education in the visual arts. My offer to teach was accepted and I enrolled for a master's degree, then a doctorate in Fine Arts and Fine Arts Education.

At first, the children and I communicated through pantomime, but when I started sketching messages, communication soared. A sketch of my family prompted sketches of their families, and soon we were sharing other experiences through drawing.

It became evident to me that the children were much brighter than their educators seemed to expect or recognize. Unable to interest educators in this school, I wrote to several psychologists, one of whom, E. Paul Torrance, sent copies of the Torrance Test of Creative Thinking, and offered to score the results. Eight of my 12 deaf students scored in the 88th percentile (compared with hearing students) in Flexibility, the 97th percentile in Fluency, and the 99th percentile in both Originality and Elaboration.

It seemed to me that we could use drawings to bypass language deficiencies and assess cognitive skills, particularly the three concepts cited by Piaget and Inhelder (1967) as fundamental in reading and mathematics: concepts of space, sequential order, and class inclusion. To develop the concepts, I asked my students to draw from observation, mix poster paints into sequences of tints and shades, and draw from imagination, offering my own sketches to those who needed help in getting started. The

Examples of stimulus drawings

popular sketches became the stimulus drawings presented in the three assessments.

An opportunity to test my theories arrived with a grant to conduct the State Urban Education Project summarized in Chapter 9. Approval for the project arrived late, after the school year had started. Since the project called for a pretest in October, and the evaluator had not yet been assigned, I was obliged to design the test items, basing them on stimulus drawings.

Subsequently, I used the test items with learning-disabled students and adult stroke patients. Eventually, my graduate students used the stimulus drawings in their fieldwork placements.

☐ Stimulus Drawings and Techniques

The first assessment, includes 50 stimulus drawings presented on 3" × 5" cards (Silver, 1981–1997). Examples are shown in Figure 2-1 and Figure 2-2. As discussed earlier, this task is based on the observation that individuals perceive stimulus drawings differently. Consider the various ways that the stimulus drawing chick was perceived and represented by different children and adults in the responses below.

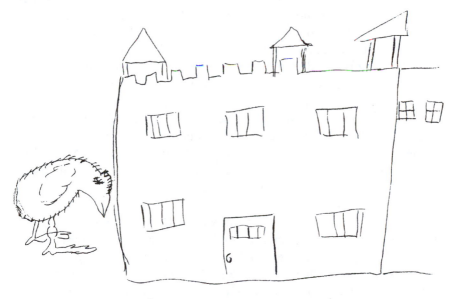

FIGURE 2-1. "A House to Remember," by Mrs. B.

FIGURE 2-2. "You'r Dead Meat," by Carl, age 8.

"A House to Remember," Figure 2-1, was the response of Mrs. B., who chose the chick together with the SD building, which others have portrayed as a castle, a prison, and a hospital. Although Mrs. B imitated the SDs, she also made an expressive change. Her chick hangs its head, suggesting the sadness implicit in her drawing and title.

"You'r Dead Meat," Figure 2-2, was the response of Carl, age 8, who chose the motorcycle along with the chick. Like Mrs. B, Carl copied both SDs, adding nothing but making an expressive alteration. His chick scowls and leans forward aggressively. Carl explained his picture as, "A giant chick the king is afraid of. The chick is running after the king" (another SD included in his story, but not his drawing).

"Growling won't help you a bit. To me your just a juicy worm," Figure 2-3, was the response of Mr. C. who selected the toothy dog in association with the chick. His drawing also shows subtle changes. Although the SD dog leads with its chest, and its leash dangles from its collar, Mr. C's dog is tethered to a stake and leans away from the chick, receding on a slant from paw to jaw. Mr. C's dog has lost its freedom and power, and in his drawing is smaller than his chick.

"There was a little bird on the tight wire in the circus and the tight wire walker wanted to save it," Figure 2-4, by Peter, age 8 associates the chick with the ladder in the context of a circus. The chick is portrayed without eyes, standing on one leg, trying to keep its balance on the wire. His chick is likely to fall, but also might be saved by the "tight wire walker." Which will it be? Peter doesn't say, but his walker has no arms or hands and is smaller than the "little" bird.

*Growling won't help you a bit.
To me your just a juicy worm.*

FIGURE 2-3. "Growling Won't Help You a Bit. To Me Your Just a Juicy Worm," by Mr. C.

Figure 2-5, "The egg can't open. Egg is break. The bird is (gestures pecking). Egg peck then open. Egg floor. The chick walk. Go away." was the response by a deaf child, Tom, age 8. He chose only one SD (he may have misunderstood the task) but related the chick to a subject of his own invention, the egg, associating it with facts rather than fantasy.

"Bird picked up the flower. Bird found money," (Fig. 2-6), was drawn by another deaf child, Marcie, age 8. Like Tom, she chose only one SD but unlike Tom, associated her chick with flowers and money. Marcie's chick has eyelashes and dainty feet, and seems feminine as well as lucky.

"The Nice Things," (Fig. 2-7) were chosen by Jimmy, age 8, who selected the SD prince and whale, together with the chick. The cognitive content of his response will be discussed later on.

These responses seem to indicate that the SD chick has different meanings for different individuals. Although some respondents associated the chick with a vulnerable young girl, as illustrated in the manual, others associated it with being male, assertive, belligerent, or with facts rather than feelings.

In this assessment, responses to the drawing task are scored on rating scales based on emotional and cognitive content. The emotional content scale ranges from strongly negative to strongly positive themes or fantasies. The cognitive scale ranges from low to high levels of ability. To avoid repetition, the scales are discussed more fully in the assessment that follows.

FIGURE 2-4. "There was a little bird on tight wire and the tight wire walker wanted to save it," by Peter, age 8.

FIGURE 2-5. "The egg can't open. Egg is break. The bird is (pecking). Egg peck then open. Egg floor. The chick walk. Go away," by Tom, age 8.

To determine the reliability of this assessment, three registered art therapists independently scored 24 responses, four drawings selected at random from each of six populations of children and adults.

In five analyses of interscorer agreement, the correlation coefficients ranged between .924 and .549. For example, a coefficient of .80 denotes 80% agreement beyond chance. Thus the scale seems to be a dependable measure for evaluating the emotional and cognitive content of responses to the stimulus drawing task by children and adults.

Studies that indicate how and why this assessment has been used in therapy, development, and assessment are summarized in this book in Parts II and III, and in the test manual.

FIGURE 2-6. "Bird picked up flower. Bird found money," by Marcia, age 8.

FIGURE 2-7. "The Nice Things," by Jimmy, age 8.

☐ The Silver Drawing Test of Cognition and Emotion

The second assessment (Silver, 1983, 1990, 1996a), is designed to bypass language in evaluating cognitive and emotional strengths that might escape detection on verbal measures; provide access to fantasies, self-images, and cognitive skills; and a way to measure individual progress. It includes three subtests: Drawing from Imagination, Predictive Drawing, and Drawing from Observation.

The SDT Drawing from Imagination Subtest

This subtest presents two sets of stimulus drawings, one for assessment, the other for use in therapy and development. Responses are assessed on quantitative rating scales for emotional content, self-image, and cognitive content.

Emotional Projection Scale

The 5-point emotional content scale ranges from strongly negative to strongly positive themes or fantasies. Strongly negative themes, such as drawings about suicide or life-threatening relationships, receive the lowest numerical score. Moderately negative themes, such as angry subjects or stressful relationships receive the next lowest score. Strongly positive themes, such as drawings about successful subjects or caring relationships, receive the highest score, and moderately positive themes, such as fortunate subjects and friendly relationships received the next highest score. The intermediate score is used to characterize ambivalent, ambiguous, or unemotional themes (neither negative nor positive or both negative and positive). The ratings are assigned numerical values, as specified in the test manual (Silver, 1996a).

"The Left-out Mouse," Figure 2-8, is a response by Jerry, age 8, a presumably typical third-grader in a public elementary school, who chose two stimulus drawings: the mouse and the cat. After finishing his drawing, he wrote the following story:

> One day a mouse went outside to play with other mice. The mice said that the mouse can't play with us. So the mouse went to bed. The next day a cat came along. The cat said that the mouse could be his friend, but the cat ate up the mouse.

Jerry's response is rated strongly negative.

The Left-out Mouse

One day, a mouse went outside
to play with other mice. The mice said
that the mouse can't play with us.
So the mouse went to bed. The next
day a cat came along. The cat said
that the mouse could be his
friend, but the cat ate up the mouse

FIGURE 2-8. "The Left-out Mouse" (strongly negative).

"The cat wants food and nobody is there to feed her and the dog scared her," Figure 2-9, was made by Gloria, age 8, who had chosen the SD cat and the refrigerator. Her fantasy about a needy and frightened cat meets the definition of moderately negative.

"High Hopes," Figure 2-10, is the response of Jennifer, a high school student, age 17, who chose the mouse and the ice-cream soda. Her fantasy is ambivalent and ambiguous. Although the mouse has high hopes, the straw seems beyond reach, and the outcome is unclear.

"Watching TV," Figure 2-11, the response by Jennifer's classmate, rated moderately positive.

FIGURE 2-9. "The cat wants food . . . dog scared her" (moderately negative).

FIGURE 2-10. "High Hopes" (Ambiguous).

FIGURES 2-11 AND 2-12. Figure 2-11 "Watching TV" (moderately positive). Figure 2-12 "Flying High with Family Love" (strongly positive).

"Flying high with family love," Figure 2-12, by a woman in a university audience rated strongly positive.

Self-Image Scale

A strongly positive self-image, such as identifying with a subject portrayed as powerful, loved, or achieving goals receives the highest score. A strongly negative self-image, such as identifying with a subject portrayed as sad, helpless, or in mortal danger, receives the lowest score. To determine self-images, respondents are asked to discuss their drawings whenever possible. A quantitative study of self-images is reviewed in Chapter 9.

Cognitive Content Scale

The scale for assessing cognitive abilities ranges from high to low levels of ability to classify—one of the three independent structures identified as fundamental in mathematics (Piaget, 1970) and in reading (Bannatyne, 1971). The concept of a class or group of objects involves the ability to select and combine into a context, such as selecting words and combining them into sentences.

According to the linguist, Roman Jakobson (1964), selecting and combining are the two fundamental operations underlying verbal behavior. Disturbance in the ability to select words is evident in receptive language disorders. Disturbance in the ability to combine words into sentences is evident in expressive language disorders.

According to the neurologist, Antonio Damasio (1994), patients with frontal lobe brain injury, may become unable to choose effectively, a defect often accompanied by a reduction in emotional reactivity. He suggests that the purpose of reasoning is to make decisions, and the essence of deciding is selecting a response option, that is, choosing a word or nonverbal action. He theorizes that the coldness of a patient's reasoning prevents him from assigning values to his options, making his decision-making flat and unemotional.

Selecting and combining also are fundamental in the visual arts and in creative thinking. Painters, for example, select colors and shapes, and if their work is figurative, they select and combine images as well. Creative individuals make exceptional leaps in selecting as well as combining their selections, and in finally representing them through images, words, or other media.

In responses to the stimulus drawing task, cognitive content is assessed for ability to select, combine, and represent ideas (creativity). Techniques for developing these abilities through drawing, painting, modeling clay, and manipulative games are discussed in Chapter 8.

Ability to Select.   Oliver and Hornsby (in Bruner, 1966) suggest three recognized levels of ability to select: The lowest is concrete, the intermediate is functional, and the highest is abstract. Up to the age of about seven, children select objects on the basis of perceptual attributes, such as color or shape (Bruner, 1966). Gradually, children take into account functions—what the objects do, or what is done to them. By early adolescence, they develop true conceptual grouping on the basis of class— invisible attributes or abstract ideas. If we ask a child in what way apples and oranges are alike, the young child is likely to say both are round. The older child is likely to say both can be eaten; the adolescent says both are fruit. Oliver and Hornsby asked for verbal responses.

The cognitive scale seeks the same information through drawings. A respondent who selects pictorial elements at the concrete, perceptual level, receives the lowest score. Those who select at the abstract, conceptual level, receive the highest score. In between are concrete selections based on function.

To illustrate, Jimmy's drawing, titled, "The Nice Things," (Fig. 2-7) received the highest score in ability to select because it represents the abstract idea of *niceness*, an invisible attribute shared by the whale, the prince, and the chick. The drawing titled "Watching TV" (Fig. 2-11) represents selecting at the functional, concrete level, and shows what the girl does.

Ability to Combine.

The ability to combine is also evaluated on a rating scale based on observations by Piaget and Inhelder (1967) who traced its development through succcessive stages. They found that children younger than seven typically regard each object in isolation. Gradually, they begin to consider objects in relation to neighboring objects, and group them on the basis of proximity and separation. Seven-year-olds begin to relate objects to an external frame of reference (e.g., the bottom of their paper), drawing a parallel base line to represent the ground, and relating their subjects to one another along this line. Gradually, their drawings become more coordinated as they take into account distances, proportions, perspectives, and the dimensions of their paper.

A response drawing receives the lowest rating for ability to combine if its subjects seem unrelated or related by proximity. The intermediate rating is received if its subjects are combined along a base line, and the highest rating is received if the drawing shows overall coordination.

"The egg can't open," (Fig. 2-5) and "You'r dead meat," (Fig. 2-2) indicate that Tom and Charlie used a base line to combine their subjects. On the other hand, Mr. C.'s drawing, "Growling won't help you a bit.," (Fig. 2-3), shows the ability to represent depth and overall coordination.

Ability to Represent (Creativity).

It is one thing to perceive an object and quite another to represent it, as Piaget and Inhelder pointed out. Children can recognize a circle long before they can draw it from imagination. To do so, they must be able to conjure up a mental image of the circle while the circle is out of sight. At first, their concepts of space are imitative and largely passive; later, they become intellectually active.

Many investigators have found that creative individuals share traits such as originality, fluency, flexibility, and playfulness (the ability to toy with ideas). Whereas analytical thinking proceeds inductively and deductively toward correct solutions, creative thinking proceeds divergently, making unusual associations.

E. P. Torrance (1980) cautioned against trying to separate intelligence from creativity, because they interact and overlap. He found that many highly creative children who performed poorly on tests of verbal ability, excelled on The Torrance Test of Creative Thinking. With his encouragement, I administered Figural Form A, of his test to 8 of my 12 deaf students. As discussed earlier, my students' scores indicated that they were highly creative compared with the norms for hearing children, scoring in the 99th percentile, for both originality and elaboration, the 97th percentile for fluency, and the 88th percentile for flexibility.

In evaluating abilty to represent, an imitative response drawing receives the lowest score if it simply copies stimulus drawings or stereotypes. It receives the intermediate score when it revises, and the highest score if it transforms stimulus drawings and is original, expressive, playful, or suggestive.

The Predictive Drawing Subtest

Predictive drawing is based on the second structure identified as fundamental in mathematics and reading—the idea of a sequence. This subtest asks respondents to predict changes in the appearance of objects by adding lines to outline drawings. Its first task evaluates the ability to predict and form a sequence which seems to develop around the age of seven.

Concepts of Sequential Order

Respondents are asked to imagine taking sips of an ice cream soda until the glass is empty, then draw lines to show how the soda would appear as it is gradually consumed. A response receives the highest rating if it represents the diminishing soda with a single series of lines with no erasures or corrections, indicating a systematic approach. A descending series of lines with erasures or corrections (indicating that the sequence was achieved through trial and error) receives the intermediate rating. An incomplete sequence, or no sequence, receives the lowest rating.

Concepts of Horizontality and Verticality

The other two tasks evaluate concepts of horizontality and verticality, or the ability to conserve, that is, to recognize constancy in spite of transformations in appearance. Most rational thought depends on this ability which appears around the age of seven (Bruner, 1966; Piaget, 1970).

One task asks respondents to show how water would appear if its container is tilted, the other asks how a house would appear if moved to a steep mountain slope. These two tasks were devised by Piaget and In-helder (1967) who observed that young children draw lines parallel to the base of the container even when it is tilted. Older children draw oblique lines which become less oblique and more horizontal, until they draw horizontal lines immediately. In addition, young children draw houses perpendicular to the slope until, eventually, they draw them upright.

In assesing these concepts, responses receive the highest rating when lines in the tilted container are horizontal, and houses on the slope are vertical, supported by posts or cantilevered (see Fig. 1-8 for an example of this). The lowest rating is given when the house is perpendicular to the slope, and when the lines parallel the bottom or side of the tilted bottle (see Fig. 1-7).

The Drawing from Observation Subtest

Concepts of space are the third of the three basic structures underlying mathematics and reading. Young children regard each object in isolation at first, then notice relationships between them. Eventually, children arrive at a coordinated system embracing objects in three dimensions.

The Drawing from Observation task is designed to measure concepts of space and the ability to represent spatial relationships in height, width, and depth. Respondents are asked to draw an arrangement of three different cylinders and a small stone. Scoring is based on the premise that respondents who represent spatial relationships accurately receive the highest score, and that lower levels can be inferred and scored. Details are provided in the SDT manual.

Reliability of the SDT

Several studies have been undertaken to determine scorer reliability. In the first study (Silver & Lavin, 1977), six judges rated pretest and posttest scores of 11 learning-impaired children. The reliability of the judges' ratings of the test results was determined by an analysis of variance (Winer, 1962). For ability to select, combine, and represent, the obtained reliability coefficient was .852. The reliability coefficient for spatial orientation was .944. The obtained coefficients indicated that the six judges had a similar frame of reference and displayed a high degree of agreement in scoring the tests.

In a second study (Silver, 1996a), seven judges blindly scored SDT responses by six children. The correlation coefficients were .93 in Predictive drawing, .91 in Drawing from Observation, and .96 in Drawing from Imagination, indicating strong reliability.

In a third study (Silver, 1996a), five judges blindly scored responses to the Drawing from Imagination task by 15 children, adolescents, and adults selected at random. Using the statistic, Intraclass Correlation (ICC), the correlation coefficients were .94 for the Emotional Content Scale, and .74 for the Self-Image Scale, again showing reliability.

In testing test-retest reliability, Moser (1980) administered the SDT twice to 12 learning-disabled adolescents after an interval of one month. All coeffiecients were significant at the .05 level of probability (.80 in Predictive Drawing, .84 in Drawing from Observation, and .56 in Drawing from Imagination.

Who can Administer the SDT?

To determine whether training is needed in order to administer and score the SDT, three studies were conducted (Silver, 1996a). None of the mental health professionals or teachers who administered and scored the SDT were trained to use it. All relied on the test manual guidelines.

In the first study, an art therapist with whom I had corresponded but never met, administered the test to 20 fourth-graders and 16 tenth-graders, and scored their responses. Then I scored the test booklets blindly. All correlation coefficients were significant; five at the .01 level (ranging between .65 and .86), and one at the .05 level (.45 in Drawing from Observation).

In the second study, another registered art therapist administered the test and scored the responses of nine mentally handicapped, hospitalized adults; then I scored the responses blindly. All correlation coefficients were significant at the .01 level (Predictive Drawing, .99; Drawing from Observation, .89; Drawing from Imagination, .91; total scores, .96).

In the third study, a classroom teacher, a psychotherapist, a graduate student in art therapy, and two art therapists scored test performances by ten children. Significant correlations were found at the .01 level (r = .66). These findings seem to indicate that training for teachers and mental health professionals is not needed.

Validity of the SDT

To determine the validity of the SDT, its relationship to ten traditional tests of intelligence or achievement were examined. Significant but low correlations were found, as reported in the SDT test manual (Silver, 1996a).

In addition, several studies found evidence of age and gender differences as well as pretest/posttest changes following art programs designed to develop congnitive skills. These studies are summarized in Chapters 9 and

10, which provides quantitative studies of responses to the assessments by typical and atypical children and adults.

Standardization of the SDT

As reported in the 1996 manual, The SDT was standardized and norms developed for cognitive scores. The scores showed gradual improvement through the school years. Additional Norms for Emotional Content and Self-Image scores are also available in the SDT Supplement (2000c).

Inter-Cultural Ideas

Information about cultural influences and universal stages of visual representation is provided in a study by Allessandrini, Duarte, Dupas, and Bianco (1998) who standardized the SDT in Brazil, based on the scores of 2,000 children and adults. They found the trend of cognitive growth similar in both cultures, increasing gradually with grade and age level. College graduates had higher scores than high school seniors. Adults with limited educations had lower mean scores than most children. In Emotional Content, they found high rates of ambivalence, and more negative than positive responses to all populations. Further information about their findings is presented in Chapter 10 (study #8).

Other findings discussed here or in the test manual (Silver, 1996a), suggest that the SDT assesses aspects of cognition that are measured to some extent by language-oriented tests, as well as the cognitive skills of respondents who rely on visual thinking as a matter of preference, or because they have difficulty putting thoughts into words, or understanding what is said.

The American Art Therapy Association gave the SDT its annual award for research in 1996. Studies of pretest and posttest changes in SDT scores following art therapy programs are summarized in Chapters 5, 6, and 9.

☐ Draw-A-Story: Screening for Depression and Age or Gender Differences

The main purpose of the Draw-A-Story (DAS) assessment is to identify respondents who may be depressed (Silver, 1993a). Form A includes 14 stimulus drawings drawn from both the SDT and Stimulus Drawings & Techniques. First published in 1988 (Silver, 1988b), it has been used as a

FIGURE 2-13. "First response by Jon, age 8, . . . he had died."

semistructured interview technique, as well as a tool to uncover masked depression. In the 1993 edition (Silver, 1993a), a second set of 14 different stimulus drawings, Form B, was added to provide a second scored response for use in therapeutic programs.

DAS is based on the theory that strongly negative responses are associated with clinical depression. The theory is based on observations by Beck, 1978; McKnew, Cytryn, and Yahries, 1983; Pfeffer, 1986; Shafer and Fisher, 1981, and others, as discussed in the DAS manual (Silver, 1993a). Like the SDT, responses are rated for emotional content and assigned numerical values. Figures 2-13 and 2-14 are examples of strongly negative responses.

Validity

The above theory was supported by the findings of three studies of depressed and nondepressed children, adolescents, and adults. The studies are summarized in Chapter 9, studies #6, 7, and 8. A brief review follows.

FIGURE 2-14. "Second response by Jon, age 10, . . . the man died."

The first study asked if there were links between clinical depression and strongly negative responses to the DAS task (Silver, 1988a). Nineteen art therapists, teachers, and school counselors in six states presented Form A to 254 children and adolescents, ages 8–21. They included respondents who were clinically depressed, normal, learning disabled, and emotionally disturbed with nondepressive psychopathology.

Approximately 56% of the depressed subjects responded with strongly negative fantasies compared with 11% of the normal subjects, 21% of the emotionally disturbed, and 32% of the learning disabled subjects. Statistical analyses indicated that the proportion of depressed subjects whose responses received the strongly negative numerical rating was greater than the proportions of normal subjects who received the strongly negative numerical rating, to a highly significant degree (chi-square

27.63, $p < .001$)—the ratings of depression subjects. The SD and LD subjects were also significant, but at the .01 and .05 levels respectively. These findings indicated that there were links between depressive illness and strongly negative responses.

The second study expanded the sample populations to 350 depressed and normal children and adults (Silver, 1988b). Twenty-four art therapists, teachers, and school counselors presented the task to clinically depressed children, adolescents, emotionally disturbed children, adolescents with nondepressive psychopathology, learning-disabled adolescents, hearing-impaired children and adolescents, and normal children, adolescents, and adults in 8 states.

As shown in Figure 2-15, approximately 63% of the depressed children and adolescents responded with strongly negative fantasies, none of the hearing-impaired children and adolescents, 7% of the older adults, compared with approximately 10% of the normal students, 13% of the depressed adults, 19% of the emotionally disturbed, and 30% of the learning disabled.

Chi-square analyses found that the proportion of depressed children and adolescents who responded with strongly negative fantasies was significantly greater than the proportion of any other group, at levels ranging from $p < .005$ to $p < .0005$. Although strongly negative responses did not necessarily indicate depression, and conversely, positive responses did not exclude depression, the findings suggested that a child or adolescent who reponds with strongly negative fantasies may be at risk. They also suggested that the DAS measure could serve as a first step in identifying some, but not all depressed children and adolescents. These findings did not apply to depressed adults, most of whom responded with ambivalent or ambiguous fantasies.

The third study asked whether self-reports or the respondents' use of space and detail would be useful in screening for depressive illness (Silver, 1993a). Subjects included 107 depressed and normal adolescents and adults.

The self-reports tended to be inconsistent with Emotional Content scores. No differences were found between depressed and normal subjects in the use of detail and space, but drawings by females showed significantly fewer details than drawings by males.

The sample of normal men and women did not differ significantly. The depressed men responded with strongly negative fantasies to a significant degree but the difference between depressed and normal men reached only borderline significance (Chi square $(1, 2) = 4.96$, $p < .05$). It was not clear whether neutral responses were associated with depression. The depressed women and girls tended to draw ambiguous or ambivalent fantasies.

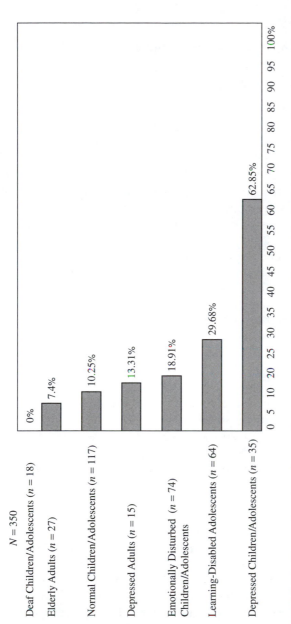

N = 350

Deaf Children/Adolescents (*n* = 18)   0%

Elderly Adults (*n* = 27)   7.4%

Normal Children/Adolescents (*n* = 117)   10.25%

Depressed Adults (*n* = 15)   13.31%

Emotionally Disturbed (*n* = 74)
Children/Adolescents   18.91%

Learning-Disabled Adolescents (*n* = 64)   29.68%

Depressed Children/Adolescents (*n* = 35)   62.85%

0 5 10 20 25 30 35 40 45 50 55 60 65 70 75 80 85 90 95 100%

FIGURE 2-15. Comparing strongly negative responses to the Draw a Story task by 350 depressed and nondepressed subjects.

Reliability

Retest Reliability

When 12 children were retested after an interval of two years, 11 of the 12 received the same scores.

At age 8 Jon drew Figure 2-13, "... he had died."

At age 10, Jon drew "The man who landed in the volcano. The man died." (Fig. 2-14).

These and the other responses seem to indicate that the negative feelings they expressed through drawings, reflect characteristic attitudes rather than passing moods.

In a second study, 12 of 24 presumably normal children who had responded with strongly or moderately negative fantasies were retested after an interval of one month. Seven of the 12 drew strongly or moderately negative responses on both occasions, 3 had higher scores, and 2 had lower scores.

In a third study, three art therapists presented DAS Form A to 31 children and adults who responded on two occasions. One therapist presented the task twice (Silver, 1993a). Their responses were identified only by a number that was assigned at random. Significant correlations were found between first and second responses (.70262, $p < 0.000$ for the first 8 subjects, and .93277, $p < .05$ for the others).

Scorer Reliability

In one study, three judges independently, and blindly, scored 20 unidentified responses to the DAS Form A set of stimulus drawings, chosen at random from four groups of children and adolescents identified previously as unimpaired, clinically depressed, learning disabled, or emotionally disturbed with nondepressive psychopathology (Silver, 1993a). Correlations between judges were significant (between judges A and B, .806, $p < .001$; judges A and C, .749, $p < .001$; and Judges B and C, .816, $p < .001$).

In a second study, two judges scored responses to the Form B set of stimulus drawings by 33 children, adolescents, and adults who responded twice without a time interval. Some were unimpaired, others were depressed, learning disabled, or emotionally disturbed. Their responses were identified only by number, and scored independently by both judges with the first and second drawings being scored on different days. Separate interscorer correlations were calculated for the first 33 responses (marked A), the second 33 responses (marked B), and the 66 combined A and B responses. Correlations again were significant. (The correlation for A scores was .83943, $p < .0.000$; for B scores, .7454, $p < 0.000$; for combined A and B scores, .80806, $p < 0.000$).

Additional studies are discussed in Parts II and III.

☐ Correlations Among the Stimulus Drawing Assessments

The three assessments use virtually the same task and rating scale to assess emotional content, but present different stimulus drawings in different arrays. This raises the question of whether different arrays of stimulus drawings affect the emotional content of responses to the task. In other words, do the assessments measure the same construct? If so, DAS users could use the DAS task to assess cognitive skills, and SDT users could use its Drawing from Imagnation task to screen for depression.

In search of answers, relationships between two of the assessments, the SDT and the DAS, were examined. It was hypothesized that the SDT and DAS do assess the same emotional and cognitive constructs. To test this hypothesis, both sets of stimulus drawings were presented without a time interval to 38 children and adults, and their responses compared. The children (7 boys and 12 girls) were between 7–8 years of age and in the second grade of a public elementary school in California. A classroom teacher administered the task, under the supervision of a registered art therapist, JoAnn Ellison. The adult sample was made up of 7 men and 12 women in a retirement residence in Florida. They had volunteered when asked to participate anonymously in a research study. Their ages ranged between "65 plus" to 85 years, with a mean age of 80.89 years.

Half the number of examinees responded first to the SDT task, then to the DAS task; the other half responded first to the DAS then to the SDT. Their scores were then correlated. The responses of both groups were scored for both emotional and cognitive content.

Results indicate that scores on both SDT and DAS assessments were correlated to a highly significant degree ($r = 0.57$, $p < .0001$), and had similar means and standard deviations. In addition, their scores followed similar patterns, as shown in Table 2-1 and Figures 2-15 and 2-16. Differences between age groups emerged, however. More that 25% of the children drew moderately positive fantasies, compared with about 8% of the adults, on both measures.

Responses for cognitive content were also significant and consistent across test scores ($r = .66$, at the $p = <.0001$). Within test scores (e.g., SDT

TABLE 2-1. Comparing SDT and DAS emotional content scores.

| | Children | | Adults | |
Score	DAS	SDT	DAS	SDT
1	5.3%	0.0	11.1%	5.6%
2	15.8%	10.6%	22.2%	22.2%
3	36.8%	42.1%	44.4%	38.9%
4	26.3%	31.6%	5.6%	11.1%
5	15.8%	15.8%	16.7%	22.2%

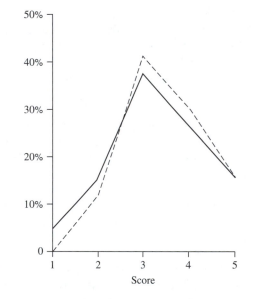

FIGURE 2-16. Comparing SDT and DAS emotional content scores of children.

Emotional Content versus Cognitive Content), no significant differences emerged.

These findings lend evidence to the validity of the emotional and cognitive content scores in both stimulus drawing measures. The size of the correlations between SDT and DAS scores suggests that the two measures assess the same constructs. The findings seem to indicate that the SDT, like DAS, can be used to screen for depression, and that DAS, like the SDT, can be used to assess levels of ability to select, combine, and represent.

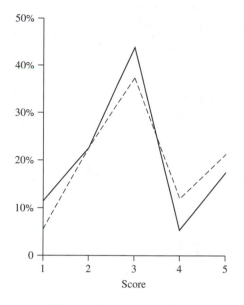

FIGURE 2-17. Comparing SDT and DAS emotional content scores of older adults.

The findings also support the view that respondents perceive the same SDs differently, creating their own interpretations and contexts. It would seem to follow that differences between the sets of stimulus drawings may be irrelevant. What seems to matter is whether the stimulus drawings provide access to an individual's fantasies, attitudes, and cognitive skills.

II

QUALITATIVE
STUDIES

Emotionally Disturbed, Hospitalized, and Sexually Abused Individuals

This chapter reviews qualitative studies of how and why the three assessments discussed in Chapter 2 were used with troubled children, adolescents, and adults in public schools, special schools, and psychiatric settings. Quantitative studies and statistical analyses of these and other atypical populations are reviewed in Chapter 9.

☐ Identifying Troubled Children and Adolescents in Public Schools

When norms were being developed for the Silver Drawing Test, it was administered to entire classes of children and adolescents in public schools. Unexpectedly, some students responded to the Drawing from Imagination task with morbid fantasies, some involving suicide; others, murder. Since it was not possible for me to conduct individual interviews with these students, they were referred for further clinical evaluation.

To illustrate how the Drawing from Imagination task has served to identify students in public schools who may pose dangers to themselves or others, this chapter begins with drawings by Alan, Rita, and Ben, who were among those whose drawings prompted referral for clinical evaluation.

FIGURE 3-1. Possessed, by Alan, age 14.

Alan

Alan, age 14, seemed a typical student in a class of 21 eighth graders in a public school in an urban, middle-class neighborhood. Academically, his score was just below the mean score for his class on the Iowa Test of Basic Skills, and just above the mean on the California Achievement Test. On the SDT, however, he received the highest cognitive score on all three subtests.

In Drawing from Imagination, Alan chose the SD knife and the bed, then made a series of drawings in which a son stabs his father to death. He titled this "Possessed" (Fig. 3-1).

Asked to respond again another day, Alan drew Murder, which showed a bank robbery, shootings, and a man wanted for murder who is caught, handcuffed, and electrocuted (Fig. 3-2).

A review of Alan's school folder indicated that his mother had remarried when he was in the 4th grade, and that he had difficulty accepting the new family situation. His mother believed this difficulty explained his poor academic performance. His fourth grade teacher described Alan as well behaved, but with unsatisfactory work. His sixth grade teacher commented that he "worked in spurts," and his seventh grade teacher conferred with his parents to discuss his study habits.

FIGURE 3-2. Murder, by Alan, age 14.

Alan's drawings suggest he identified with the murderer who is possessed by the devil and kills his father, as well as with the bank robber who murders and is sentenced to death. Compare Alan's drawings with those of his classmates.

Max drew, Panic in a Church, after selecting the bride and the mouse (Fig. 3-3). He seems to have used aggressive humor, and enjoyed the embarrassment of the bride and the consternation of wedding guests. Academically, he performed at the12th grade level on the Iowa and California tests. On the SDT, he did not do as well as Alan but came close.

Another classmate, Sarah, responded with Going to the Malt Shop, (Fig. 3-4). She seems to identify with her subject enjoying a soda. Although she scored at the 11th grade level on both the Iowa and California tests, her Drawing from Imagination was functional and unimaginative, and her total SDT score was well below the mean score for her class.

Why did Alan receive high scores on the SDT but moderate scores on the Iowa and CAT, compared with Max and Sarah? A possible explanation is that Alan was a gifted underachiever, performing at grade level academically, but preoccupied with conflicting wishes and fears,

FIGURE 3-3. "Panic in a Church," by Max, age 14.

FIGURE 3-4. At the Malt Shop, by Sarah, age 14.

while his classmates were also gifted but not burdened with emotional distress.

Rita

Rita, age 10, also seemed typical of the children in her fourth grade class, scoring at the fourth grade level on the Metropolitan Reading Instructional Test. Her teacher described her as "normal with average intelligence."

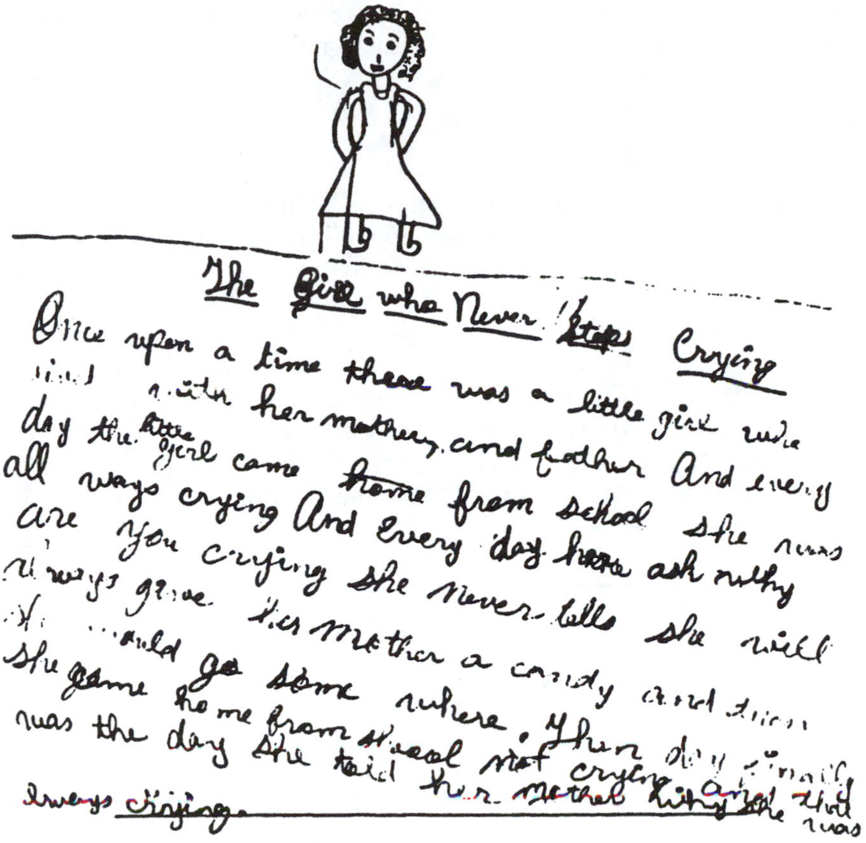

FIGURE 3-5. The Girl who Never Stops Crying, by Rita, age 10.

For the SDT, she chose only one stimulus drawing, the girl, drawing her with averted eyes, and hands behind her back. She gave her drawing a title, The Girl who Never Stops Crying (Fig. 3-5) then wrote the following story:

> Once upon a time there was a little girl who lived with her mother and father. And every day the little girl came home from school she was always crying. And every day her ask why are you crying? She never tells. She will always give her mother a candy and then she would go somewhere. The day finally she came home from school not crying and that was the day she told her mother why she was always crying.

Rita's fantasy was not violent but strongly negative nevertheless, and seems to represent herself. Although its cognitive score placed her in the 6th percentile, her scores in Predictive Drawing and Drawing from

Observation placed her in the 14th and 11th percentiles, suggesting that Rita, like Alan, was preoccupied with emotional problems.

Ben

Ben, age 14, had poor motor coordination and expressive language impairments. According to his teacher, he had few friends and was shy, polite, and withdrawn. When his parents were divorced, he remained with his mother.

One day, Ben spontaneously drew two fantasies about buildings on fire. In both drawings, Ben asks his father for help. In the first, Ben says, "Daddy my house is on frie help me." Daddy replies, "Don't cry/pull the fyre alarm box." In the second drawing, Daddy replies, "I'm coming."

I showed Ben's drawings to administrators and the consultant psychiatrist in his school, but they did not take his drawings seriously until the

FIGURE 3-6. The Dying Bride.

following week when Ben was apprehended walking in the midst of traffic on a city bridge.

Other Children and Adolescents

Compare the following responses by presumably normal adolescents with responses by adolescents previously diagnosed as clinically depressed.

The Dying Bride, Figure 3-6, was drawn by another of Alan's eighth grade classmates; Figure 3-7, was drawn by a 15-year old youth diagnosed as clinically depressed, attending a special school for emotionally disturbed children.

Beach Monster Eats Surfer!!, Figure 3-8, was drawn by a sixth grader in the public school, who chose the dinosaur; Figure 3-9, Delicious Corporal,

FIGURE 3-7. Drawing by a Clinically depressed 15-year-old.

FIGURE 3-8. Beach Monster Eats Surfer!!, by a sixth grader.

was done by a clinically depressed youth who also chose the SD dinosaur, adding the following story:

> Corporal Kristy had just passed an airborne test and ready for the real thing. On a Monday morning, Kristy and other jumped an air force plane. Kristy jumped and he saw a monster mouth. Oh shoot he blew aire and cooked me in the air. He ate me and felt contented.

Similarities between the responses by adolescents previously diagnosed as clinically depressed, and the strongly negative responses by Alan, Rita, Ben, and others, suggest that all were suffering from depression, both diagnosed and masked. This hypothesis has support in the DAS validity studies summarized in Chapter 2.

FIGURE 3-9. Delicious Corporal, by a clinically depressed youth.

☐ Using the Assessments in Special Schools and Hospitals

The following sections describe how and why stimulus drawing assessments are used with emotionally disturbed children and adults in special schools and hospitals.

Peggy Dunn-Snow, PhD, ATR-BC, LPAT

Dunn-Snow (1994) described her use of the Draw a Story (DAS) assessment to determine the needs of severely emotionally disturbed students in the elementary and secondary schools of a large urban school district. After a high school student expressed self-destructive thoughts in responding to the drawing task, she checked school records and discovered that he had a history of clinical depression. She then used art therapy to help him resolve feelings about the death of his father.

She also used the DAS task to break down resistance among students who previously refused to participate in school art therapy sessions, and with other students who became anxious when asked to do free-choice artwork. She found that DAS provided enough structure and support to enable them to begin making art in therapy sessions.

In addition, Dunn-Snow adapted the task for group art therapy with boys in the fifth grade to resolve conflicts, provide structure, and set limits, inviting each boy to choose a stimulus drawing and then collaborate with others. The boys combined their images into a single drawing with a common theme, title, and story line. She observed that in accomplishing this task, they followed directions, accepted limits, solved problems, made compromises, and communicated effectively.

Christine Turner, ATR-BC

Turner (1993) discussed her use of DAS as part of a five-drawing assessment series with adolescent clients in a psychiatric hospital setting. She used response drawings to assess the probability of a client's history of abuse, and if such a history existed, to assess the extent of abuse, the meaning the client attached to the abuse, and the effects of the abuse on the client's defenses, coping skills, sense of self, relationships, and world view. She then made treatment recommendations to assist ward therapists in working with the client, and also made after-care recommendations, as needed.

Turner's sequence of five drawings were Free Subject, Scribble Drawing, Kinetic Family Drawing, Self-Drawing, and Draw a Story, Form A. The DAS was placed last because she found that its more cognitive nature provided closure. The themes, which emerged in the DAS drawings, confirmed impressions derived from the preceding four drawings as well as other sources. Occasionally, adolescents who produced four guarded stereotypical images, showed greater freedom in working with DAS and in metaphorical story telling. Conversely, clients who accessed and expressed painful feelings might use the DAS to regroup and condense the content of the other four drawings into a safely distanced metaphor. She found areas of greatest need depicted and described in DAS responses. Attributions of causality, locus of control, concerns about self-protective abilities, trust/mistrust, self-values, and community attachments were suggested by these responses and became topics for discussion. Whether the client remained metaphorical or related the DAS drawing to events in his or her own life, Turner found opportunities to begin addressing treatment needs, confirming reality, and laying the groundwork for future therapy.

Cathy Malchiodi, ATR-BC

In her book, *Breaking the Silence* (1997), Malchiodi described using the stimulus drawing task as a projective technique to minimize uneasiness and anxiety in working with children and adolescents who had been sexually abused. She discussed the response of a 13-year-old girl who had been abused for at least five years by many of her mother's boyfriends. The girl chose and drew the boots, then dictated a story expressing fear, about sleeping in a haunted house, and receiving warning notes that had suicidal connotations.

Malchiodi found the task helpful in obtaining critical information for structuring immediate intervention for the child. As she points out, art therapists who work with children suspected of being sexually abused, are often concerned with how to interview when the goal is possible disclosure. She also found communication through art less traumatic than verbal communication, and that children express themselves more readily through art activities.

In her second book, *Understanding Children's Drawings* (1998), Malchiodi observed that children's own narratives, rather than symbols or specific art elements, may reveal depression. She found four themes particularly important in their narratives and the content of art expressions: isolation, despair, mourning/bereavement, and destructive or self-destructive themes. Children often express one or more of these themes in their drawings and their narratives.

Louise Sandburg, ATR

Sandburg used the 50 stimulus drawing cards in working with hospitalized schizophrenic adults (Sandburg, Silver, & Vilstrup, 1984). Her instructions to the participants were to choose two or three cards and think of a story that could include them. These instructions remained the same from week to week in order to establish consistency. She encouraged her clients to create their own imagery, rather than copy the stimulus drawings, as recommended in the scoring guidelines, and found that copying became an issue when a patient who insisted on copying first joined the group, or was in regression.

Sandburg displayed finished drawings on a wall to encourage socializing, then asked questions. She presented art experience as a problem-solving task in order to make the process of drawing attractive to those with poor self-concepts. She found that the stimulus drawings served to focus fragmented thinking and provide pleasure. After working with the stimulus drawing cards for a year, her patients decided to construct their own "story cards."

Felix Carrion, ATR

Carrion (Silver & Carrion, 1991, p. 42) used the SDT and DAS in an inpatient psychiatric program as part of a battery of tests to obtain information about the resources patients brought to treatment. His findings modified previous assumptions about the ability of patients to sequence, organize, predict, and conceptualize visual information. He presented the history of a patient who was unable to predict a sequence. As he observed, it would have been easy to assume the patient's difficulty had a psychological origin, such as resistance to disclosure, whereas responding to the drawing task revealed "a deficit in organizing the sequence of visual material in a way that makes sense." He also described a 12-year old girl whose ability to fantasize was picked up in her responses to the drawing tasks.

Mary F Wilson, ATR

Wilson (1990) used the DAS assessment to gain insight into the emotional outlook of depressed, suicidal, and hospitalized adolescents, as well as for insight into how the sense of self and environment were evolving. She administered the task to eight patients during the first session of a biweekly treatment program, and again three months later. Of 13 responses to the task, 12 had moderately negative and severely frightening elements whereas one response was positive. Wilson observed that DAS provided information about emotional states, and how patients viewed their situations.

Kristen Vilstrup, ATR

Vilstrup, Sandberg, and Silver (1984) used the stimulus drawings as a projective technique in her work with adolescents in an inpatient psychiatric setting. Finding that the drawings stimulated the formation of symbols, she used the symbols of her patients as metaphors to develop insight into their strengths, conflicts, and maladaptive defenses. She concluded that keeping her interpretations within the metaphor, that is, speaking in the child's symbolic language, enabled her to offer healthier coping choices.

Vilstrup described changing a child's drawing of a dragon pursuing a helpless victim by adding a fence to contain the dragon, thus helping him alleviate a threatening situation and set healthy limits. She found that the SDs provided opportunities to enter into a child's symbolic language, and that the story-telling process provided insight into strengths and weaknesses, enabling her to facilitate conflict resolution.

Joey, a Child with Learning Disabilities

This chapter describes the use of stimulus drawings by a remediation teacher in Canada, Ms. O, who had asked if she might participate informally in a project conducted in New York (Silver, 1983a). The project was designed to improve the cognitive skills of an experimental group of children legally designated as learning disabled or emotionally disturbed, or performing at least one level below grade level, and was supported by a grant from the National Institute of Education. Ms. O and I arranged that she would work along with the Project's art therapists using the same procedures with one child weekly for 12 weeks, supervised via telephone and correspondence.

The child she chose, Joey, age 8, had been diagnosed as learning disabled and assigned to a behavior modification program. In the second grade of a public school, he had difficulty learning to read and tended to "lash out at his peers, sometimes justified but often uncalled for." As measured by the Canadian Cognitive Abilities Test (CCAT), his IQ was 91, below average. Only two of the 24 children in his class had lower scores. As measured by the SDT Drawing from Imagination subtest, he received the highest score in his class in cognitive skills (99th percentile). The emotional content of his drawing was strongly negative, and he received the lowest score in Drawing from Observation (14th percentile).

To clarify the relationship between the two tests, the scores of both were analyzed. Correlations were found between the CCAT and Drawing from

FIGURE 4-1. The Killier, by Joey, age 8 (pretest).

Imagination at the .01 level of significance ($r = .50$). No significant correlations were found between the CCAT and Drawing from Observation.

Except for Joey, most of the children in his class performed as well in Drawing from Imagination as on the CCAT. The three children with the next highest scores in Drawing from Imagination had IQ scores ranging between 123 and 150 on the CCAT.

Joey's pretest Drawing from Imagination, The Killier (Fig. 4-1), seems to represent a doctor operating on a patient who calls for help although anaesthetized. Upstairs, someone lies in bed, snoring. Even though Joey's teacher did not ask him to talk about his response, his title suggests he is able to select at the abstract level (because he used the word "Killer," which Webster's New World dictionary defines as one who kills habitually). In ability to combine, his drawing goes beyond the base line level typical of 8-year-olds (someone is upstairs). In ability to represent, it is highly expressive and suggestive. Although strongly negative in emotional content, it is not clear if he identifies with the victim, the smiling Killier, the sleeper above, or the narrator of his story.

The following week when Joey responded to the Drawing from Imagination task, he selected stimulus drawings of an elephant and an old tree, then drew The Elephant's Journey, Figure 4-2. Birds are nesting and the elephant is smiling as it walks toward the tree. With time for another

FIGURE 4-2. The Elephant's Journey, by Joey, age 8.

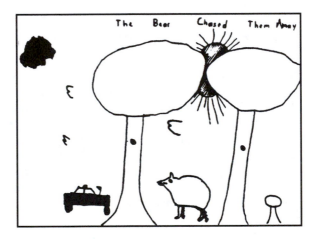

FIGURE 4-3. The Bear Chased Them Amay, by Joey, age 8.

drawing, Joey selected the whale and the alligator, then drew them confronting each other with clouds over heads, "The Fight is Going to Begin" (perhaps having second thoughts).

The third week, Joey drew, "The Bear Chased Them Amay," (sic), Figure 4-3. The bear stands between two trees. A red car with yellow flag and blue roof lamp (a police car?) is behind the tree, facing the bear, and a dark blue cloud floats above. Joey's title seems to express a wish, contradicted by his drawing. It suggests the trees frustrate the bear, as they block the sun.

The next meeting called for mixing poster paints into tints and secondary colors, then painting from imagination. Drawing from observation followed painting, followed by modeling clay, family portraits, and self-portraits (Joey drew himself smiling). These developmental procedures are presented in Chapter 8.

During the art program, the CCAT was administered again, scheduled annually in his school. Joey's performance gained 8 points (from 91 to 99) while the mean score of his 24 classmates decreased from 113 to 108. According to Ms. O, his classroom teacher felt that he had "improved almost 100%, adding, "you have Joey all turned on these days, he is so thoroughly enjoying his experiences."

Then a series of unfortunate events began to unfold. Joey's classroom teacher threatened to cancel the art program because he misbehaved. She then cancelled two sessions. Ms. O became ill and postponed their meetings for 5 weeks. She saw him two weeks before the school year ended for the last time. She presented the stimulus drawings, then administered the SDT again as a posttest.

Seeing an Elephant in the Woods! Figure 4-4, is Joey's last drawing before the posttest. After selecting the mountain climber and the elephant, he drew a climber, without ears and wearing dark glasses, climbing a tree, his back to the elephant. Like his previous drawings, trees block the elephant's progress, and for the first time, a cloud extends across the sky.

Again, Joey's drawing contradicts his words: The climber could not possibly see the elephant behind him, and trees would hide the elephant from the airplane above, even if Joey had given the plane windows. His drawing suggests that he identifies the elephant with himself, invisible and isolated in the forest. Like his pretest drawing from imagination, this

FIGURE 4-4. "Seeing an Elephant in the Woods," by Joey, age 8.

FIGURE 4-5. "The Dog Chasing the Cat," by Joey, age 8 (posttest).

drawing scored in the 99th percentile, suggesting that Joey's expressiveness remained intact, and that he remained troubled by feelings of frustration.

Joey's posttest Drawing from Imagination, "The Dog Chasing the Cat," Figure 4-5, shows several noteworthy differences from his pretest. His score declined, placing him in the 83rd percentile in cognitive content. In emotional content, it no longer reflects a painful world. Although chased by the dog, the cat does not seem to be suffering. His ability to represent spatial relationships shows remarkable gains. He drew a house in the background, a wall in front of the house, a tree in front of the wall, and the chase in front of the tree—concepts of depth unusual for an 8-year-old. His gain in ability to combine was offset by losses in ability to select and to represent. He seems to have selected on the functional level, simply showing what dogs and cats do. Furthermore, they seem static and unemotional, compared with his pretest drawing. His posttest score in Drawing from Imagination dropped to the 91st percentile, down from the 99th percentile of his pretest.

In Drawing from Observation, Joey's posttest improved greatly, scoring in the 85th percentile. His pretest drawing had suggested deficiencies in visual memory or perception. In his posttest drawing, spatial relationships were accurate in height, width, and depth. His Predictive Drawing score did not change, remaining slightly below the mean score of his classmates.

Was art experience responsible for Joey's gains and losses? Was the individual attention he received from Ms. O responsible for his gains?

TABLE 4-1. IQ Scores for Joey and two matched classmates.

	1979	1980	1981
Joey	91	99	90
Timothy	97	90	79
Lewis	87	83	90

Was his decline in expressiveness the price paid for gains in spatial skills? Unfortunately, there are few answers.

I wrote to Ms. O during the summer recess, but received no reply. When I learned that her phone number had been assigned to someone else, I wrote to the school's principal who replied that Ms. O had died.

A series of letters with her colleagues ensued, keeping me informed about Joey's progress during the next five years. In March, 1981, the CCAT was again administered by a new special education teacher. Previously, in 1979, before the art program, Joey had been matched with two classmates who did not share his art program experience. The children were tested again in 1980, after Joey had attended four or five art sessions, and finally, in 1981, about a year after the program ended. Joey's IQ score on the CCAT increased during the art program, but when it was administered the following year, his score had dropped back to 90, as shown in Table 4-1.

In November 1983, Joey's 6th grade teacher wrote that Joey's "frustrations with learning had reached a point where he took out his frustrations in the form of general misbehaviors," and that he had frequent misbehaviors in grade 5 and grade 6. His grade equivalent scores on standardized tests were at the 3rd and 4th grade levels in subjects such as reading, spelling, and arithmetic.

In March 1984, I received a letter from another teacher who wrote that Joey's progress had been very good, and his behavior exceptional. "His parents and teachers comment on how mature he acts." This teacher felt that there were several reasons for the changes in Joey's behavior and academic ability: a new teacher, a split grade 7/8 class, remedial assistance, and the introduction of a computer which Joey had adopted. This teacher wrote, "His parents have purchased one and he has devoted much of his energies into computer work."

In addition, the SDT had been administered. Joey's performance at age 13, showed virtually no changes in cognitive skills, placing him at the 65% percentile in Drawing from Observation and the 72nd percentile in Drawing from Imagination, based on the 6th grade norms.

Stay Away from House!! Figure 4-6, is Joey's Drawing from Imagination at age 13. It shows both changes and consistencies in emotional content.

FIGURE 4-6. "Stay Away from House," by Joey, age 13.

Instead of representing himself as an elephant or bear thwarted by external restraints, he seems to represent himself as a dog, restrained by a leash tied to a dog house, but defending his home, his TV, his flag, and his food dish which seems to be named, "bear." In his drawing, Joey's environment remains hostile but he has replaced the trees that blocked and isolated him at age 8, with evergreens behind the doghouse, and a leafless tree behind the hissing snake. The dog and doghouse may reflect low self-esteem but also the growing maturity mentioned by his teacher—the dog effectively defends himself and his possessions.

The developmental techniques used by Ms. O are presented in Chapter 8. The National Institute of Education Project and quantitative studies of other learning disabled students are reviewed in Chapter 9.

CHAPTER

5

Hearing-Impaired Children and Adolescents

This chapter is concerned with four hearing-impaired children who responded to the stimulus drawing tasks. Burt and Vi were among the children chosen at random for the experimental group of the State Urban Education Project discussed in Chapters 2 and 9. Lisa and Charlie participated in other art programs.

Children who cannot learn language in the usual way are often deficient in cognitive functioning. It is generally assumed that the cause of their deficiency is language retardation, and that the only remedy is to develop verbal skills. When we are preoccupied with their limitations, we lose sight of their strengths. Some skills develop in spite of impairments. Others develop *because of* impairments. As Rene Dubos observed, one of the most important laws of biology is that the many potentials of a cell usually become manifest only when it is compelled to use them. The many potentials of children also may become manifest only when disabilities compel their use. One such potential is the visual-spatial intelligence that is evident in visual art forms.

☐ Burt

Burt, age 13, had severe hearing loss (75 dB in his better ear) as well as receptive and expressive language disorders. His performance on the

FIGURE 5-1. A face the author drew for Burt.

Stanford-Binet test indicated that at age 7, his mental age was 3 years, one month.

Burt participated in 9 of the 11 sessions of the art program. In the first, he chose the boy and the knife from an array of stimulus drawings. He drew a faceless boy, and asked me how to draw a face. I started to demonstrate on the blackboard, but Burt made it clear that he wanted me to draw his face on a sheet of paper, which I did (Fig. 5-1). He then added a face to the subject of his drawing, a large knife across the stomach with what may be a skull and bones on the knife handle, airplanes, buildings, a car with windows suggesting eyes, and finally, what seems to be smoke over the car and blood on the knife (Fig. 5-2). When the session ended, Burt was so engrossed that his classroom teacher offered to let him stay until he had finished.

At our second meeting, Burt again chose the boy and the knife but drew airplanes dropping bombs on ships and buildings (Fig. 5-3). Although both drawings are strongly negative, the subjects of his first drawing seem unrelated, and the man and knife are larger than the car and buildings. In his second drawing, however, he related the planes to their targets with

FIGURE 5-2. Burt's first drawing.

FIGURE 5-3. Burt's second drawing.

conventional symbols—dotted lines and scribbles, perhaps to represent smoke.

Our third meeting began with a demonstration of mixing poster paints into secondary colors (see Chapter 8). Burt worked hard but his hands trembled, and his attempts to retrieve drops of paint with his palette knife only made matters worse.

FIGURE 5-4. Burt's third drawing.

At our fourth meeting, I introduced clay, starting with a technique for helping children learn to conserve, that is, recognize that an object remains the same in spite of transformations in its appearance (Sonstroem, 1966). Burt apparently learned to conserve. He had been one of 11 nonconservers on the pretest, and one of four conservers on the posttest three months later. He also modeled his lump of clay into a box with a slit on top—a bank. He was so delighted with his bank that he refused to wait until it was dry, taking it with him.

At our fifth meeting, stimulus drawings were presented again. Burt chose the head-and-shoulders sketch of a nurse, but drew her full length with crutches (Fig. 5-4). Unlike his previous, fragmentary drawings, this drawing is organized in form as well as content. His nurse fills the paper as though its edges served as frames of reference, and the crutches suggest that Burt had a story in mind.

With time to spare, Burt painted a house, tree, clouds, and raindrops, using black paint and a few touches of red and blue. As he finished, he began to talk about his painting, and I wrote his words on the blackboard. He copied them spontaneously on his painting, "No cars, no people, rain all over, can't walk, get a boat, swim."

The last meeting began with a demonstration of Drawing from Observation. Burt's drawings are shown in Figure 5-5. His first drawing (A), shows that he failed to represent height, width, and depth. In his second drawing (B), he represented these relationships correctly but omitted the toy bug. Before he began his third drawing (C), I asked him to change places with a classmate on the opposite side of the arrangement. Apparently, the reversals confused him, and two of his cylinders seem to float above the table.

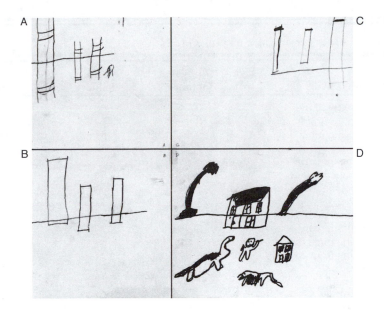

FIGURE 5-5. Burt's responses to Drawing from Observation. A) shows a lack of height, width, and depth; B) represents correct relationships; C) illustrates view from the other side & the table; D) is Burt's last drawing from observation one week later.

For his last drawing, a week later (D), Burt drew a landscape consisting of a toy house, animals, and trees. He represented the objects and spatial relationships accurately, although his trees are above the top edge of the base plane.

Since I did not call attention to mistakes, Burt's gains seem to reflect his own observations and corrections. His drawing suggests he had reached Piaget's Stage 3, typical of children his chronological age (Piaget, & Inhelder, 1967, p. 432).

Before the art program began, I had asked his classroom teacher to evaluate his abilities using a 5-point rating scale. She gave him the lowest score, "almost never," for ability to select named objects or combine words into sentences. She also gave him the lowest score for ability to group objects on the basis of class, to associate new information with what he knew, and to conserve (did he know that spreading out a row of pebbles does not increase the number of pebbles?). She repeated her evaluation when the art program ended, three months later, and again six months later, at the end of the school year. Although her evaluation was subjective, it parallels and supports the findings of the project's pre- and posttests, which eventually developed into the SDT. As shown in Table 5-1, out of

TABLE 5-1. Burt's performance on project tests.

Cognitive Skills	Pretest October	Posttest January	Changes
1. Conserving liquid	0	5	**+5**
2. Conserving solids	0	5	**+5**
3. Conserving numbers	5	5	0
4. Ordering a series	5	5	0
5. Ordering a matrix	3	5	**+2**
6. Ordering colors	1	5	**+4**
7. Placing objects in given positions	3	5	**+2**
8. Horizontal orientation	3	5	**+2**
9. Vertical orientation	5	5	0
10. Grouping three objects	3	3	0
11. Grouping from an array	5	3	**−2**
12. Selecting	1	5	**+4**
13. Combining	1	5	**+4**
14. Representing	1	5	**+4**
mean	2.57	4.71	2.17

a maximum score of 5 points, Burt's mean score on the pretest was 2.57; on the posttest, 4.17.

☐ Vi

An eight-year old boy, Vi had receptive language impairments and severe sensori-neural hearing loss secondary to maternal rubella. With a hearing level of 76 dB in his better ear, he had profound speech and language delays, secondary to his hearing loss, as well as disorders of the central nervous system. According to school records, his intelligence was above average.

Vi's responses to the Drawing from Imagination task seem to reflect emotional changes as well as changes in cognitive skill. In his first drawing, a woman and animal are inside a house, the woman's arm is raised as though she was about to throw something, and three unrecognizable objects seem to float outside (Fig. 5-6). Since Vi did not want to discuss his drawing, his intention is unclear.

For his second drawing, he chose three stimulus drawings—the bug, the mouse, and the man seated on a chair. He drew them along the bottom of

FIGURE 5-6. Vi's first drawing.

FIGURE 5-7. Vi's second drawing.

his paper, the man at one end calling, "mouse, bug." Vi also included his name after the mouse at the end of the line (Fig. 5-7).

The third week, when painting techniques were demonstrated, Vi shouted, "green!" when he saw yellow being mixed with blue. He did not try to mix his own colors, however; instead, he drew a boy, painted the boy's face and shoes yellow, and the ground, blue, then added, "Vi Me." The absence of hands suggests that Vi feels helpless, but even though small, Vi has placed himself at center stage (Fig. 5-8).

The following week, Vi chose a man, explaining that the man is a magician holding an egg, which had been inside the hat on the table (Fig. 5-9).

FIGURE 5-8. Vi's third drawing.

FIGURE 5-9. Vi's fourth drawing.

For the first time, Vi discussed his artwork and mixed colors on his palette, producing green for the ground (representing magic?).

Figure 5-10 began as an imitation of a classmate's painting of a boy and girl fishing from a boat. The classmate's boy says, "I love fishing," the girl says, "me too," Vi's girl (larger and with green hair) says, "I got fish," the boy says nothing.

FIGURE 5-10. Another drawing by Vi.

FIGURE 5-11. A strongly positive drawing by Vi after the art program ended.

I intervened, saying, "Vi, you don't have to copy Dave. You have great ideas of your own," whereupon Vi wrote his name in the sky, in formations of flying birds.

Vi's drawings, paintings, and signatures suggest a growing self-confidence. His schoolwork also improved, and during the spring semester, he spent part of each day in a public school, ending his participation in the art program.

One day, Vi visited the art class, and joined in Drawing from Imagination. Choosing the dinosaur, he painted, Figure 5-11. The small human figure at the lower right seems to have shot the dinosaur to save the building, perhaps a metaphor for himself as a hero triumphing over misfortunes. This last response about achieving goals, is strongly positive, as measured by the emotional projection scale.

Vi's cognitive performance on the Project's pretest and posttest also showed gains, improving from the lowest score on the pretest to the highest score on the posttest in Ability to Select, Combine, Represent, and order a series of colors, as well as in art skills. It also showed moderate gains in horizontal and vertical orientation. On the Torrance Test of Creative Thinking, his scores increased from 47% to 55% in Fluency, and from 46% to 50% in Elaboration.

On the other hand, Vi showed little or no gains in Conserving Liquid, Conserving Solids, Transposing a Matrix, or Ordering a Series of Sticks. On the Torrance Test, he did not improve in Originality or Flexibility.

☐ Lisa

Lisa responded to the drawing tasks while participating in experimental art classes in a school for deaf children. Her drawings illustrate the observation that some deaf children spontaneously use drawings to achieve a sense of control. Children who are inarticulate tend to have difficulty persuading others or making their wishes known. By altering the appearance of the subjects they choose, they can punish villains, ventilate anger and fear, and change painful experiences into pleasant ones, if only vicariously.

Lisa's painting, The Spook, Figure 5-12, seems an attempt to experience control by altering an unpleasant experience. She had visited an amusement park, and after riding through a dark tunnel, suddenly arrived at a frightening tableau. As she explained, she is the small figure below the cage, saying, "help me." By putting the spook behind bars, she changed her frightening experience into a safe one.

Lisa seemed to use drawing and painting to share personal experiences. In Figure 5-13, for example, she pointed out that the person in the coffin was her grandmother and that the figure on the right was herself in a swimming pool (Silver, 1978, 2000b).

Lisa's classroom teacher became so intrigued by her drawings that she asked Lisa to bring them with her when she returned from the art sessions. During the weeks that followed, Lisa's drawings and paintings became increasingly impersonal, culminating in a painting of three rectangles, titled, Hotel/2 Pools. When I asked Lisa if anyone could swim in her empty pools, she answered, "No. The pools are closed."

Thereafter, Lisa's artwork remained in the art room, and her enthusiasm for drawing personal events returned. One drawing shared information

FIGURE 5-12. The Spook, by Lisa, age 10.

about dental braces, how much they cost, and how they look both off and on the teeth. In her final drawing at the end of the school term, she portrayed an event that occurred at the school picnic when a classmate suddenly lost his lunch.

☐ Charlie

Charlie and I first met when he was 11-years-old, attending an art program in another school. He had spent a year in a mental hospital when he was six, but the following year, a psychiatrist found him "not psychotic, not schizophrenic, not autistic," but suffering from receptive and

FIGURE 5-13. A drawing by Lisa, age 10, that allowed her to share personal experiences.

FIGURE 5-14. A drawing by Charlie, age 11.

expressive language impairment with a high degree of selectivity for excluding sounds.

Since he did not talk in the art classroom, we communicated through pantomime. Charlie was enthusiastic and quick to learn. His gesture for pleasure was kissing his fingertips in salute, and he often saluted his brushes and paints. One of his drawings, Figure 5-14, became the logo for an exhibition circulated by the Smithsonian Institution (Silver, 1976).

We met again three years later in another art program. At age 14, Charlie had been assigned to a class for slow-learners in another school. In this later art program, Charlie drew variations of his earlier pictures (Fig. 5-15 and also Figs. 5-16 and 5-17). His landscape of leafless trees and broken

FIGURE 5-15. A drawing by Charlie, age 14.

FIGURE 5-16. A drawing by Charlie, age 11.

branches was quite unlike the verdant landscape he had painted when he was 11.

Charlie's sister told me that he was unhappy in school, "came home wild," and refused to do his homework. I also learned from the school's psychologist that Charlie's intelligence had not been tested because his language skills were inadequate.

Charlie's spatial intelligence, however, like his art skills, seemed to be extraordinary. For example, our art group visited a museum, which provided a diagram of its galleries, and Charlie led the way because he could read the diagram even though it was upside down in my hand as we walked.

FIGURE 5-17. A drawing by Charlie, age 14.

I discussed this with the school psychologist, but she was not impressed. As she explained, "language comes first, and there's a limit to what can be done without language." Unable to interest her in testing Charlie, I wrote for guidance to E. Paul Torrance who sent the Figural Form of the Torrance Test of Creative Thinking and offered to score the results. As he wrote, Charlie's performance reflected "a high order of ability to acquire information, form relationships, and in general to think." Charlie had scored in the upper 5% in Originality, the upper 3% in Fluency, the upper 10% in Flexibility, and in Elaboration, his score was "almost unexcelled" when compared with test norms. Subsequently, I presented the Torrance Test to other hearing-impaired students, most of whom received high scores, as discussed in Chapter 2.

What are the limits to what can be done without language? A search for answers led to the writings of Piaget, Langer, and other investigators, as discussed in Chapter 1, and eventually to developing the SDT. By then, Charlie was a young man. He agreed to take the test, and as I hoped, received the highest score on each subtest.

Recently, two studies found the SDT performances of hearing-impaired children equal or superior to the performances of hearing children. These studies are summarized in Chapter 9.

6

CHAPTER

Adults and Adolescents with Brain Injuries

This chapter discusses how and why the stimulus drawings were used with brain-injured patients in hospitals and outpatient facilities. The patients responded to stimulus drawing cards as well as the Silver Drawing Test and DAS assessments.

☐ Mr. O

At the age of 56, Mr. O had suffered a cerebral hemorrhage. Although discharged from the hospital, he returned once a week to a rehabilitation center for therapy. According to his speech therapist, he had both expressive and receptive language impairments. He spoke fluently but did not always make sense. He tended to confuse grammar and verb tenses, and could not read aloud. He also had difficulty following a series of directions, such as "Put the book on the table, and the pencil in your pocket." According to the medical report, he found expressing concepts particularly difficult.

Asked to clarify his expressive disabilities, and ease them if possible, I used the SDT Drawing from Imagination task as pretest and posttest in our first and last meetings. At other times, I presented various combinations of stimulus drawings.

Mr. O performed well in Drawing from Observation and Predictive Drawing on the pretest, but in Drawing from Imagination, his response

FIGURE 6-1a. A Life Time of Growth, by Mr. O (his first Drawing from Imagination).

FIGURE 6-1b. Cat and Dog Competition in Strange Home, Mr. O.

was confused. He selected the man and the woman, then drew, A Life Time of Growth, Figure 6-1a. It shows no interaction between subjects, receiving a low score in Ability to Select. It uses stereotypes and stick figures combined with arrows, and received low scores in both Ability to Combine and Ability to Represent. His total score in Drawing from Imagination placed him in a percentile that was comparable to performances by children in the second grade, as measured by the SDT norms. In Emotional Content, his drawing seems unemotional, neither positive nor negative, receiving the intermediate score.

Mr. O's second response, Cat and Dog Competition in a Strange Home, Figure 6-1b, also was comparable to the performance of children ages 7 to 8. It was unclear whether his score reflected cognitive or language disorders, perhaps both.

I hoped to encourage Mr. O to express concepts and feelings visually through drawings, as well as verbally, through titles and conversation. We met four times in weekly, hour-long sessions.

For our first meeting, I spread stimulus drawings on the table, people and animals in one cluster, places and things in the other. Mr. O selected the mountain climber, then drew, Gathering Magic Herbs, (Fig. 6-2). In his drawing, he changed the mountain climber from a child to an adult with rope, axe, and flask. His climber is higher than the airplane, and has nearly reached the mountaintop. On a neighboring peak, a mountain goat seems to be eating—magic herbs? Mountain climbing is an appropriate metaphor for trying to recover one's health, and the message suggests a wish-fulfilling fantasy.

FIGURE 6-2. Gathering Magic Herbs, by Mr. O.

At our second meeting, Mr. O selected the whale and the seascape, then drew, Call Home Quick. There is a Whale in Sight (Fig. 6-3). His choice of a whale with water spraying from its spout is another fitting metaphor, symbolizing a cerebral hemorrhage. In trying to explain his drawing, he pointed to the figure on the dock and said, "sing walk walk." I asked if he meant telephoning. He said, "yes," that someone is telephoning his wife and children to tell the news, adding that his words, "did not come out right." He then talked about the onset of his stroke while having lunch with a friend. Suddenly, he found himself unable to talk. When he picked up pencil and paper, he found himself unable to write. Nevertheless, he was aware of what was happening, not only then but also throughout his stay in the hospital, even though he remained unable to talk.

The following week, Mr. O chose the city street, then made two drawings: one of people with canes and crutches, titled, Handicapped People that can be Trained to new Aspects of Machine Maintenance; the other of a pedestrian following dotted lines across city streets, titled, Paths to Learning Machine Maintenance. He then talked about his work as an executive

FIGURE 6-3. Call Home Quick. There's a Whale in Sight, by Mr. O.

in a large company, and mentioned that he planned to return to work soon. Although the subjects of his drawings had difficulty walking rather than talking, and their work involved maintaining machines rather than maintaining communication, they seemed to represent himself. Like his mountain climber, his subjects tend to be overcoming obstacles, pursuing goals, and finding their way through a maze of streets, surrogates for himself trying to overcome his disabilities.

At our last meeting, Mr. O responded again to the Drawing from Imagination task. As in the pretest, he chose the cat but this time, associated it with the snake. In his posttest response, Hedges may Hide Surprises, the snake turns away from the cat, perhaps retreating into the hedge (Fig. 6-4). The cat, facing the snake, resembles the stimulus drawing cat with arched back and tail raised; however, the eyes of Mr. O's cat are open and it seems to smile. Perhaps Mr. O was preoccupied with returning to work the following day, representing himself as a cat able to intimidate the snake even though surprised by its unexpected appearance. On the other hand, he might have identified with a surprised and retreating snake. Mr. O offered no explanation, choosing to spend the rest of our meeting saying goodbye. His posttest scores showed gains in ability to select, combine, and represent; in emotional content his drawings remained ambiguous.

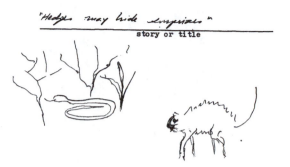

FIGURE 6-4. Hedges may Hide Surprises, by Mr. O (his last Drawing from Imagination).

Mr. O's visual and verbal responses seem to indicate that his impairments were linguistic rather than cognitive. They also suggest that art experience provided opportunities to express indirectly the fears and wishes he did not, or could not, put into words.

☐ Jim

Jim had suffered a stroke at the age of 18, just after graduating from high school. Three years later when we met, he remained paralyzed on his right side. He had learned to draw with his nondominant left hand, and had just applied to the State Office of Vocational Rehabilitation for assistance in attending art school. He was a shy and withdrawn young man who spoke slowly in incomplete sentences.

Since his expressive language impairment was more severe than his receptive impairment, I was asked to evaluate his nonverbal, expressive abilities and limitations, in order to clarify his potentials for commercial art.

As measured by the SDT, he received the highest possible score in two of the three subtests, Drawing from Imagination and Drawing from Observation, but performed poorly in Predictive Drawing.

Jim also responded to the set of 50 stimulus drawings. For his first response, Jim chose a tree and a woodland landscape. Although the SDs include three trees—one leafy, one leafless, and one gnarled—Jim chose only the leafless tree, centering it in a mountain landscape, titled Reservior in the Catskills where I go Fishing, Figure 6-5.

The branches on the left side of Jim's tree are upright, like the SD tree; on the right side, however, they slant at a lower angle, suggesting the paralysis of own right side. As Jim described this tree, it was "in the dormant stage." Then he added trees behind it, the branches of the evergreen on the left pointing up; on the right, the branches point down. Asked if he could

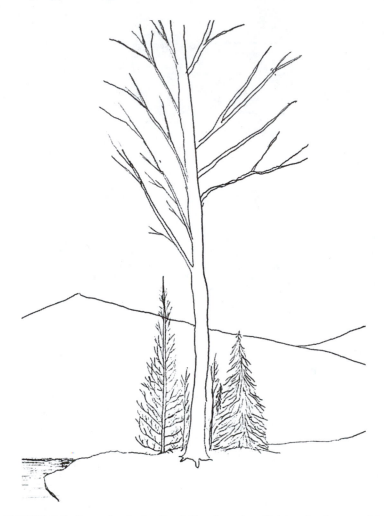

FIGURE 6-5. Reservior in the Catskills where I go Fishing, by Jim, age 21.

put himself in the picture, Jim hesitated, erased some lines, then added another tree in the background.

When we met again, Jim chose the stimulus drawing fish, changing it into a "Salmon, a Cohoe," (Fig. 6-6) then with pastels, drew, The Cohoe got Away, Figure 6-7.

In a subsequent drawing, Jim again chose the leafless tree together with the boy and man, then drew, Keep Out/Ice, Figure 6-8. The boy seems to be rescuing the man who has fallen through the ice, pulling him to safety with a rope. Leafless trees and a car on a distant road complete his landscape.

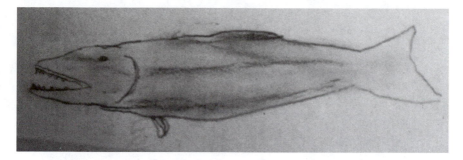

FIGURE 6-6. A Salmon, a Cohoe, by Jim, age 21.

FIGURE 6-7. The Cohoe got Away, by Jim, age 21.

In responding again to the drawing task, Jim chose the ladder, the man, and the boy and drew, Carrying a Child Down a Ladder/Helping Somebody, (Fig. 6-9).

In my report, I indicated that Jim's hesitant speech and slow movements obscured an alert mind, that his impairments did not carry over to his

FIGURE 6-8. Keep Out, Ice, by Jim, age 21.

artwork which showed high levels of skill, and I recommended training in commercial art. I was unable to persuade the Office of Vocational Rehabilitation, however, and three years later, Jim remained unemployed, living at home with his parents.

☐ Gary

At the age of 15, Gary had suffered a stroke that left him unable speak and paralyzed on both sides of his body, with movement limited to two fingers of his left hand. He was one of eight patients in a study to determine whether the art procedures would be useful in evaluating and developing the cognitive skills of stroke patients who had varying degrees of language impairment (Silver, 2000c). Gary seemed the most severely impaired in terms of motor capacity, yet he was the only patient able to perform all the tasks presented to him. He could not sit unsupported, and because he had difficulty swallowing, he could not prevent saliva from escaping from his mouth. He seemed to understand everything I said, however, and although he could not speak, he communicated by pointing to letters of the alphabet printed on a board in his lap. To signal the end of a word, he tapped the bottom of the board as though it were the spacebar of a typewriter. Although he could not sit unsupported in his electric wheelchair,

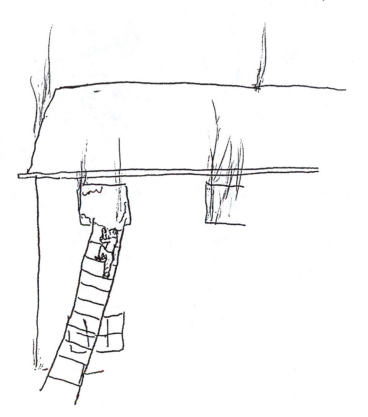

FIGURE 6-9. Carrying a Child Down a Ladder/Helping Somebody, by Jim, age 21.

he maneuvered it skillfully, and responded to the drawing tasks with enthusiasm.

In drawing from observation, a felt-tipped pen held between his two functioning fingers, Gary included not only the cylinder arrangement, but also the table where it was placed, other objects on the table, and a nearby chair (Figure 6-10). This drawing indicated that he was able to perceive and represent spatial relationships in height, width, and depth, suggesting that his ability to draw from observation remained intact.

In drawing from imagination, he chose a stimulus drawing car, then drew two cars, one above the other. Using the cartoon device of a balloon around the upper car to indicate that it was lower car's dream or fantasy, he also spelled out his title, Dreaming About a Dune Buggy, Figure 6-10.

The idea of a car dreaming about another car suggests that Gary was alert and imaginative. The dreaming car, its headlights and tail lights turned on, is green; the dreamed car is red, the complementary color. Above it

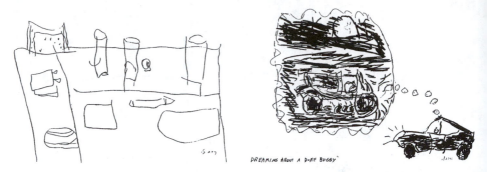

FIGURES 6-10 AND 6-11. Figure 6-10. Drawing from Observation, by Gary. Figure 6-11. Dreaming about a Dune Buggy, by Gary.

is the moon in a dark sky. We may speculate that the lower car, asleep and dreaming about its opposite, could symbolize Gary's immobility and yearning for romance.

Gary's ability to represent his thoughts through drawing from imagination also seemed intact. His abilities suggest his disabilities may have been due to subcortical damage rather than cortical lesions. If so, Gary's response drawings suggest that drawing may be of value in helping to localize the areas of brain damage.

Unlike Gary, the other patients were unable to perform many of the drawing tasks.

☐ Mrs. V

Mrs. V was unable to do any of the tasks. An inpatient in a wheelchair, she was a woman in her thirties, paralyzed on her right side and unable to speak. Her receptive language remained unclear. She seemed unable to understand the drawing tasks, but when I spread a group of tinted cards before her on the table, she moved them into a sequence of colors. On the other hand, she seemed unable to place sticks in order from short to long.

Reluctant to give up, I moved my chair to sit beside her rather than across the table, and, placing her hand over mine, sketched the figure of a man, omitting the face, then offered my pencil. She scribbled on the face. I then drew other incomplete human figures and each time, she scribbled the body parts I omitted, such as ear, foot, or arm. She also tried to retrace some of my pencil lines (see Fig. 6-12).

Encouraged, I began to sketch Mrs. V. She held still as though posing, watching my pencil as it moved across the paper. After finishing the sketch,

I offered her the pencil and a blank sheet of paper. She then drew the smiling face (see Fig. 6-13).

There were too many variables to determine what enabled Mrs. V to progress from scribbling to drawing. It may have been because watching a sketch of herself intrigued her, or because I was beside her rather than across from her, or because she had sufficient time to associate the moving pencil with the lines it produced.

☐ Mrs. J

This young woman had recovered from her stroke except for difficulty in using verbs. Like the verbs missing from her sentences, actions and interactions were missing from her drawings. She performed the Predictive Drawing and Drawing from Observation tasks without difficulty. In Drawing from Imagination, however, she chose the apple, banana, and two people with arms around each other, then copied them as isolated objects unrelated in size or placement (see Fig. 6-14).

I asked if she could draw the apple the way it would appear in the hand, then placed in her hand the stone from the Drawing from Observation arrangement. First, she added the jagged line to her sketch of an apple, then extended the hand of her incomplete human figure, adding fingers and the apple (see Fig. 6-15).

☐ Mrs. M

An in-hospital patient whose recent stroke left her unable to talk and paralyzed on the right side, Mrs. M easily performed the Drawing from Observation and Predictive Drawing tasks. In Drawing from Imagination, however, she performed poorly.

At our first meeting, she selected three stimulus drawings: the car, the hammer, and the man, then drew them one above the other, as shown in Figure 6-16. In cognitive content, her drawing received the lowest scores in Ability to Select, Ability to Combine, and Ability to Represent. In Emotional Content, it is ambiguous and unemotional.

To encourage Mrs. M. to draw relationships between her subjects, I sketched a man breaking a car window with a hammer, then offered other stimulus drawings. She chose the man, motorcycle, and dinner tray, but again drew them in isolation. When I asked if she could show how they might be related, she added lines to the human figure suggesting arms reaching toward the tray (Fig. 6-17).

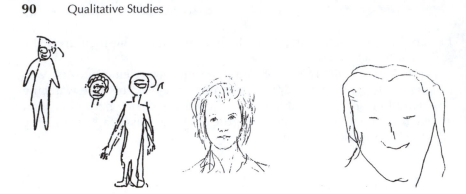

FIGURES 6-12 AND 6-13. Figure 6-12. Drawing from Imagination, by Mrs. V. Figure 6-13. Portrait sketches.

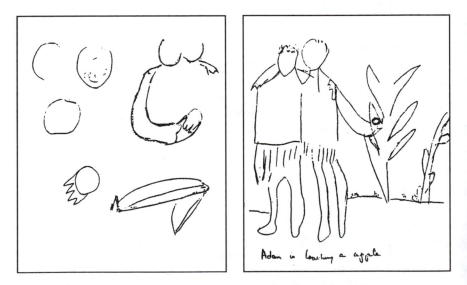

FIGURES 6-14 AND 6-15. Figure 6-14. Drawing from Imagination, by Mrs. J. Figure 6-15. "Adam is touching a apple" by Mrs. J.

FIGURE 6-16. Mrs. M's first Drawing from Imagination.

Mrs. M's receptive language seemed intact, like her ability to select subjects to draw. Her impaired ability to combine seemed to extend beyond language to nonverbal expression through drawing, to synthesizing parts of her drawing into an integrated whole. During our ten weekly meetings, I tried to encourage her to show relationships between the stimulus drawings she selected. For example, when she selected the dog and the man, drawing them side by side, I copied her drawing but added a leash, linking the man's hand to the dog's collar. She reinforced my pencil line with her pen, spontaneously, then drew the banana in the man's other hand (Fig. 6-18).

At our last meeting, Mrs. M. again selected the man together with the interior of a room, then drew the man's arm reaching toward a phone (Fig. 6-19). This drawing suggests some gains in Ability to Select (her subjects are related on the basis of function) and Ability to Combine (her drawing shows depth). In Emotional Content, it is moderately positive, the man smiles as he reaches toward the phone (will he call her? Is she calling him?).

FIGURE 6-17. Mrs. M's second Drawing from Imagination.

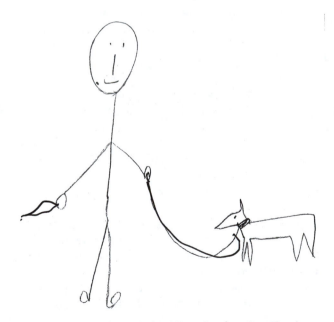

FIGURE 6-18. Mrs. M's third Drawing from Imagination.

FIGURE 6-19. Mrs. M's fourth Drawing from Imagination.

These findings raise the question whether gains in ability to select, combine, and represent through images will carry over to gains in expressive language, or vice versa. This question remains unexplored.

☐ Assessment of Brain-Injury Patients

In a presentation at the 1993 Conference of the American Art Therapy association, Mary F. Wilson discussed her work with inpatients and outpatients who had sustained brain injuries in accidents, assaults, strokes, and aneurysms. She used Form A of the Draw-A-Story instrument to assess her patients' skills and emotional outlooks. Presenting the stimulus drawings mounted on a cardboard background, she asks her patients to identify each image to assess word-finding and speaking ability. To assess their ability to establish relationships and to create and organize images, she asked them to combine subjects in drawings and show something happening between them. She also examined executive functioning, reasoning, problem-solving abilities, and field neglect problems which became evident if the patient drew closer to one side of the page or the other. During the story writing stage of the task, she observed reading and writing skills.

As a member of the clinical treatment team trying to assess a patient's strengths and weaknesses, Wilson used this assessment as a component of her art therapy evaluations. She found that it served to reinforce the findings of other therapists, and introduced new information in many instances. Usually the Silver instrument confirmed information about physical and cognitive functioning already discovered by other clinicians. However the drawn assessments contributed unique information about emotional outlook and depression, fantasies, and image-creating abilities. Since information on emotional outlook was an especially valuable contribution to the team, this became the focus of my study. (Wilson, 1993)

Wilson observed that her patients most frequently choose the SD volcano, castle, dead tree, cat, chick, and mouse. She also noted that the volcano paralleled her patients' focus on their brain injuries and emotional outbursts. The castle seemed to symbolize the hospital or home to outpatients as well as inpatients. The dead tree symbolized the loss of limb functioning as well as life before the injury. The angry cat apparently suggested dark emotions and bad luck. Occasionally, the cat's female image was significant. "The mouse and chick were often selected to serve as the projected self, corresponding to the low self-esteem and diminished sense of personal power" (Wilson, 1993, p. 10).

As a whole, Wilson's brain-injured patients rarely drew strongly negative or strongly positive fantasies, scored 1 and 5 points respectively. Their scores tended to cluster between 2 and 4 points, possibly because the patients were protected from extremes due to medication and increased safety precautions.

Wilson found that the DAS assessment provided information without being tedious for the participants to complete, and that her patients almost always projected themselves into their drawings and stories, offering material about their emotional inner lives, such as issues of low self-esteem, concerns about adjustment to disability, and depression over losses.

CHAPTER 7

Uses of Humor

This chapter begins with observations about the kinds of humor expressed by children, adolescents, and adults in response to stimulus drawing tasks, and presents examples of the kinds of humor found. Although most responses are not humorous, those that are, provide access to defenses, anxieties, and desires. The chapter concludes with studies of age and gender differences in the use of humor.

Avner Ziv (1984) suggested five functions of humor. An aggressive function helps us hide aggression by expressing it in a socially acceptable way. It enables us to feel superior and to punish others. Humor also serves a defensive function, helping us face reality, see the danger, challenge it, and achieve a sense of mastery. It enables us to challenge fears, withstand threats, relieve tension, avoid depression, and deny dangers by making them appear ridiculous. It includes self-disparaging humor, which serves to win sympathy or admiration, and lessen anxiety. An intellectual function gives new meanings through incongruity or absurdity meant to amuse. The fourth function, sexual humor, allows us to deal openly with a social taboo; and the fifth, social humor, such as satire, provides social acceptance.

Several of these functions have appeared in responses to the Drawing from Imagination task. For example, aggressive humor seems to take two forms.

☐ **Lethal Humor**

Some respondents use strongly aggressive humor that results in death, and seem to expect the viewer to share their amusement. To illustrate, John, age 18, chose the stimulus drawing dinosaur and mouse, and then made a series of drawings titled, "Godzilla Vs Mighty Mouse," Figure 7-1. After they meet, Mighty Mouse leaps into the air flying "at the sound of speed," Godzilla bites off its tail off, Mighty Mouse prays and forgets about Godzilla. Godzilla does not forget Mighty Mouse, however, and gobbles him up "in one chomp." John seems to identify with Godzilla, and expect the viewer to share his amusement.

Humorous fantasies about destroying someone may serve to mask intense anger, or desire for revenge, perhaps a warning of potential violence, or the surface expression of underlying depression. On the other hand, drawings about victims portrayed as ridiculous, embarrassed, frightened, or unfortunate in other ways, may be used to mask frustration and desire to punish.

FIGURE 7-1. "Godzilla Vs Mighty Mouse," by John, age 18.

☐ Disparaging Humor

A moderate form of aggressive humor seems aimed at others in a mean-spirited way, an invitation to laugh at someone else's discomfort or misery, hiding a desire to humiliate or punish rather than destroy. An example is shown in Figure 7-2, titled, "Life Experience, the seat of applied learning," by someone in an audience of art therapists. Another example, "Panic in a Church," by Max, age 13, was shown in Chapter 3 (Fig. 3-3).

Some respondents use Disparaging Humor to ridicule themselves, demonstrating Ziv's observation that self-disparaging humor serves defensive purposes. We joke about our own anxieties, or joke about frightening situations to make them ridiculous. Consider the response by Mrs. A, an elderly woman who used the first person singular in her title, indicating that the subject of her drawing was herself. She selected and copied two stimulus drawings, a fish and a person leaning on an elbow, then wrote, "I am a Pisces. So where is the other fish?" (Fig. 7-3).

This drawing suggests that Mrs. A feels lonely and abandoned, but by making herself ridiculous, and joking about loneliness and frustration, arouses sympathy and admiration.

FIGURE 7-2. Life Experience, the seat of applied learning, by a young man.

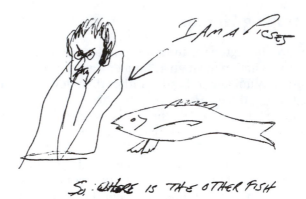

FIGURE 7-3. "I am a Pisces. So where is the other fish?" by Mrs. A.

FIGURE 7-4. Mr. W's use of humor.

Humor directed toward one's self can serve as a defense by winning sympathy and reducing anxiety. Like Mrs. A, Mr. W seems to identify with his ridiculous and unfortunate subject. He chose the stimulus drawings of a man with raised fist, and associated him with a defiant horse. In his drawing, the man says, "Gid-a-up, Bronco." The horse replies, "Sez who?" (Fig. 7-4). Mr. W invites us to join him in laughing at the frustrated man who seems to represent himself.

Like Mr. W and Mrs. A, Mr. M. had volunteered to participate in a study as part of a program provided by a charitable organization that provided hot lunches to seniors living in a low-to-middle socioeconomic urban neighborhood in New York. The volunteers and I met one afternoon

FEAR OF ANIMALS

FIGURE 7-5. Fear of Animals, by Mr. M.

after lunch. After looking over the stimulus drawings spread on a cafeteria table. Mr. M chose the sword and the elephant, then drew, "Fear of Animals," Figure 7-5. His elephant, challenged to a duel by an old, ridiculous artist, smiles and looks away as though rolling its eyes. Mr. M's drawing suggests that he used humor to confront a fear with an absurd fantasy, and hopefully, achieve relief.

☐ Resilient Humor

A similar form of humor has become evident in responses to the drawing task. Like self-disparaging humor, it addresses unpleasant realities, but differs by creating amusing ways to outwit the cause of distress and achieve favorable results. Consider the drawing titled, "She is riding the subway with security, saying, 'Now they can't snatch my gold chain,'" (Fig. 7-6), the response of a young woman in a college audience who chose stimulus drawings of a woman and a snake. Her response suggests that she fears being robbed and wishes for security. She seems to have used humor to relieve her anxiety by fantasizing about a way to make her gold chain (and herself) safe.

Joe, 17, who chose the dinosaur and the mouse, drew the sequence shown in Figure 7-7. His mouse, hands clasped, gazes upward; the huge foot descends, the mouse struggles, lifts the heavy weight, overthrows the dinosaur, and has the last laugh. Joe seems to identify with his mouse, and to expect the viewer to applaud its courage and strength.

☐ Ambivalent or Unclear Humor

Still another form of defensive humor seems characterized by ambivalence. For example, consider the drawing titled, "Queen on a Leash,"

FIGURE 7-6. 'Now they can't snatch my gold chain', by a young woman.

FIGURE 7-7. Mouse overturns Dinosaur, by Joe, 17.

FIGURE 7-8. "Queen on a Leash," by a young man.

Figure 7-8, by a young man, whose title contradicts his drawing. He may have meant to be amusing, or his words could have been a slip of the tongue. Nevertheless, his drawing reveals that the queen, not the dog, holds the leash, suggesting that the young man may have anxiety about his relationship, and fears losing control.

☐ Playful Humor

This kind of humor seems to have no hidden agenda, but is motivated by feelings of well-being and good will, meant to be absurd, amusing, and shared.

Max, age 14, chose the stimulus drawing of children peering from a window, and a farm landscape. In drawing, he brought the children outdoors, gave them bodies and an amusing ride, then titled his drawing, "Jig-a-did-dig 2 kids on a pig!" (Fig.7-9).

Mrs. B, an elderly woman, chose the stimulus drawing parachutist and dinosaur, then drew, "Return from Outer Space," Figure 7-10.

Mrs. B and Max seem to have enjoyed drawing their fantasies, and invited the viewer to share their enjoyment.

Studies of Age and Gender Differences in the Use of Humor

Two previous studies found that a sample of senior adults, more than other age groups, responded with humorous drawings to a degree that was statistically significant, (Silver, 1993b and c, reviewed in Chapter 10). The purpose of the studies had been to determine whether there were

FIGURE 7-9. Jig-a-dig-dig 2 kids on a pig!

significant age or gender differences in attitudes toward self and others, and had examined the responses of 531 children, adolescents, and adults to the Drawing from Imagination task. One finding indicated that the senior adults expressed more negative attitudes than any other age group, and that many of their negative responses used self-disparaging humor. Although responses by senior men were more negative than responses by senior women, they used humor more often.

The present study was an attempt to amplify and verify these findings by reexamining responses to the SDT Drawing from Imagination task by 215 females and 169 males who had no known impairments. They included 53 girls and 61 boys ages 9 to 12; 73 girls and 73 boys ages 13 to 19; 62 women and 18 men ages 20 to 50; and 27 women and 17 men ages 65 and older.

Teachers and art therapists had administered the tasks to the children and adolescents in public schools in New Jersey, New York, and Pennsylvania. I had administered the task to adults in Florida and New York who volunteered to respond anonymously.

Comparing age groups and gender groups in the various uses of humor, the numbers were too few to be meaningful. Consequently, uses of humor

FIGURE 7-10. "Return from Outer Space," by Mrs. B.

in responses to the Draw A Story task were also reexamined and the results combined.

The DAS respondents included 248 females and 217 males in the same age groups as the SDT respondents. The sample of children consisted of 45 girls and 41 boys ages 9 to 12; the adolescents, 97 girls and 131 boys ages 13 to 19. The samples included 177 with no known impairments, and 151 who were emotionally disturbed. Thirty teachers or art therapists administered the DAS to the emotionally disturbed children and adolescents in hospitals or special schools, and to unimpaired children in public schools in New Jersey, New York, Minnesota and Ohio.

The sample of adults included 35 women and 28 men ages 20 to 64; and 71 women and 17 men ages 65 and older, who volunteered to participate anonymously. They resided in Florida and New York, and I administered the task.

☐ Results

Of the 849 respondents to both tasks, 141 made humorous drawings (16.61%). The largest proportion of respondents who made humorous

TABLE 7-1. Uses of humor in responses to the SDT and DAS drawing from imagination tasks.

Age Group	Number Using	Lethal Humor	Disparaging Humor	Ambivalent or Unclear Humor	Resilient Humor	Playful Humor
9–12	18	7	7	1	1	2
13–19	73	31	29	4	1	8
20–50	33	5	13	5	3	7
65+	17	2	11	1	1	2
Totals	141	45	60	11	6	19
		(31.91%)	(42.55%)	(7.80%)	(4.26%)	(13.48%)

drawings used Disparaging Humor (43%), followed by approximately one third who used Lethal Humor (32%). Of the remaining responses, 14% expressed Playful Humor; 8% Ambivalent Humor, and 4% Resilient Humor, as shown in Table 7-1.

Although age and gender differences also emerged in the kinds of humor used, the number of respondents is too small to justify useful observations. It is hoped that future studies with larger population samples and responses to the set of 50 stimulus drawings, will provide worthwhile information.

CHAPTER

Developmental Art Procedures

This chapter presents the objectives and procedures that were used to help some of the children discussed so far—Joey, Burt, Vi, and Charlie—develop cognitive and creative skills. These procedures were also used with children who had no disabilities, and with the other children and adults who had learning disabilities, hearing-impairments, or brain injuries, as discussed in Chapters 5, 6, 7, and 9. The procedures were field tested and validated in three projects (Silver, 1973; Silver & Lavin, 1977; Silver et al., 1980) discussed in Chapter 9.

☐ Objectives

The stimulus drawing approach to art therapy has four objectives: to expand the range of communication, to invite exploratory learning, to present tasks that are self-rewarding, and to build the self-esteem of children like Mike (See Chapter 2), who lack confidence in themselves.

Expanding the Range of Communication

We used art procedures as a way to communicate effectively, emphasizing content rather than form. We showed children how to draw, paint, and model clay to enable them to give form to experiences they could not put into words, and share these experiences with others. Some spontaneously used poster paints in thin washes as though they were watercolors, while others used them thickly, as though they were oils. Some chose broad brushes; others preferred brushes with fine points. These individual differences were encouraged.

Inviting Exploratory Learning

We encouraged the children to experiment with their art tools and materials, hoping this would help them discover mistakes, and correct them. Instead of pointing out errors, we offered suggestions on scrap paper.

Providing Tasks That are Self-Rewarding

Work that demands the greatest effort can be the most rewarding. Art experiences can be so rewarding that they are sometimes considered play instead of learning, but they also provide unique opportunities for quiet reflection and the reveries that often accompany art experiences. The pleasures of overcoming obstacles, and losing one's self in work, can be healing in themselves without our interventions. We tried to protect the children from interruptions, including our own, but interceded when the children's lack of skill threatened to defeat their intentions, such as struggling with a brush that was too large, too small, too wet, or too dry.

Building Self-Confidence

Art experiences can provide special opportunities for both building the self-confidence of a child with low self-esteem and tearing it down. The subjectivity of a painting makes the painter particularly sensitive to criticism and curiosity. Unlike a daydream, a fantasy on paper is vulnerable to anyone who sees it and feels qualified to judge. Children like Lisa are likely to withdraw, or conceal their feelings and fantasies. Building self-confidence does not require indulgence or insincere praise. Appreciating subjective qualities in artwork is valuing the person who creates it.

☐ Developing Ability to Sequence and Conserve

The following media can be used to help develop the abilities of sequencing and conservation.

Paints

Materials: Poster paints in red, blue, and yellow (the three primary colors from which secondary colors can be mixed) as well as white and black; paper palettes (or cafeteria trays covered with white paper), sheets of paper (12 × 18 inches or 18 × 24 inches), palette knives, paper towels, one-inch and pointed brushes, water dishes, and sponges for cleaning up.

In advance, set a place for each participant, providing a palette, palette knife, broad brush and pointed brush, sheet of paper, and paper towel. After participants arrive, demonstrate mxing a series of tints on your palette (using a palette knife) by adding more and more white to a dab of blue poster paint.

Next, ask participants to put dabs of white and a chosen color in the upper left and right corners of their palettes, and mix a sequence of tints between them. Subsequently, ask them to add the remaining primary colors to other corners of their palettes, and create sequences (and tints) of the secondary colors—purple, orange, and green.

After this introduction, encourage them to discover and invent colors of their own by painting images or abstract designs. Whenever more of one color is added to another, a sequence is formed. Later, provide black paint so that they can create shades as well as tints.

Figure 8-1 shows the painting materials the children used. On the left in Figure 8-2 is the palette of a child who was able to create sequences of color; on the right, the palette of a child who had not learned.

FIGURE 8-1. Painting materials.

FIGURE 8-2. The palette of a child who was able to create sequences of color (left). The palette of a child who has not yet learned this task (right).

Modeling Clay

Materials: Clay and modeling tools (or pencils, paper clips), a piece of wire for cutting clay, paper towels, and plastic bags for storing sculptures. For each participant provide two flat sticks approximately 12 × 1 × 1/4 inches, and a wooden roller, approximately 12 inches.

In advance, prepare a fist-sized lump of clay and provide modeling tools for each participant as well as yourself. You might start by asking participants to hold the lump of clay in both hands, eyes closed, and experiment by pulling, twisting, and hollowing the clay, then try modeling it into forms.

To develop ability to sequence, demonstrate rolling a small lump of clay with the palm of your hand on the table until it becomes a ball. Then invite participants to make a series of larger or smaller balls, or other forms.

The "slab" technique can be useful in developing ability to conserve. Begin by rolling a lump of clay between parallel sticks, both ends of the roller resting on the sticks. Slice off uneven edges, and roll again until the slab becomes a rectangle which can be cut into smaller rectangles and pinched together to form a box, house, or some such three-dimensional form. Keep your demonstrations brief, just long enough to convey the basic technique.

☐ Developing Concepts of Space

The following procedures were used to stimulate perception of spatial relationships in height, width, and depth.

Drawing from Observation

Materials: An orange or small ball, cylinders made by rolling and taping sheets of construction paper in various colors, pencils with erasers, crayons or markers, and drawing paper that is approximately 8 1/2 × 11 inches.

In advance, place the orange and one (or more) cylinders on a sheet of paper in the center of a round table, or another table surrounded by desks and chairs. This arrangement should be below eye level so that the paper is seen as a plane rather than a line. Place the objects side by side on the paper, one further forward than the other.

Demonstrate drawing the arrangement, including the paper base, from observation, then ask participants to draw the arrangement as it appears from their different points of view. Instead of pointing out mistakes, call attention to spatial relationships (e.g., the orange is in the foreground and to the left of the ′cylinder, when viewed from here, but in the background and to the right, when seen from there). As participants finish sketching, ask them to exchange seats with others who have finished, so that each can sketch the arrangement from different points of view.

It is helpful to sit beside a participant who finds it difficult to draw from observation, his or her point of view. Then sketch the arrangement slowly, calling attention to the line formed by the back edge of the paper base which provides a frame of reference.

In later sessions, you might try portraits, toy landscapes, and still-life arrangements, including groups of sculptures.

Calling attention to spatial relationships, encouraging observation, and providing time to draw without interruption, can prompt exploratory learning and the spontaneous correction of mistakes. To illustrate, Figure 8-3 shows the progress of Ben, age 14, who had exceptionally poor visual-motor coordination.

Manipulative Games

We also used a task suggested by Piaget and Inhelder (1967), building two identical toy landscapes on cafeteria trays. These landscapes included mountains modeled from plaster and embellished with rivers, paths, matchstick trees topped with balls of clay, and toy houses, cars, and people. On one of the landscapes, 17 numbers were added.

One player is asked to place a car in the same position as a car on the numbered landscape, and to continue matching the position of the other car as it is moved to another numbered position. After a few trials,

Ben's first attempt, drawing an arrangement of three cylinders and a toy bug

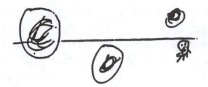

Ben's second attempt, drawing a toy landscape.

Ben's third attempt, drawing the same arrangement of cylinders and toy bug.

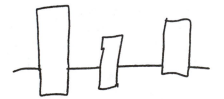

FIGURE 8-3. Drawings from Observation, by Ben, age 14, who had expressive language impairments and poor visual-motor coordination.

the unmarked landscape is turned 180 degrees, requiring the player to match locations that are reversed on the other player's landscape. The game proceeds from positions 1 to 17, each location increasingly difficult to find.

Other manipulative games designed to sharpen awareness of spatial relationships are discussed later in this chapter.

FIGURE 8-4. An example of a manipulative game, building identical toy landscapes.

I found it useful to join in art-making from time to time. Body language, like words, can communicate art techniques and the pleasures of drawing, painting, and modeling clay.

Provide frequent opportunities to select and combine colors, shapes, and subject matter while Drawing or Painting from Imagination.

Emphasize content rather than form, meaningful pictures rather than abstract designs, exploratory learning rather than directive teaching, and eliciting responses rather than instructing.

☐ 12-Session Art Program

This art program was the program used in the National Institute of Education Project discussed in Chapter 9; see Silver et al., 1980.

The program presented here includes objectives and procedures for the first 12 sessions. Subsequent sessions should be based on the review of each student's strengths and weaknesses, and should either repeat specific procedures or adapt them to individual needs.

If the SDT is used before and after the program to note changes in ability, a minimum of 12 sessions (40 to 60 minutes) should be planned. Preferably, for handicapped students, the program should continue throughout the school year.

In addition to the specific objectives and procedures presented on the following pages, there are six general objectives and procedures, indicated below, appropriate to all the sessions.

Objectives	Procedures
1. to develop cognitive skills	
a. focus attention	set limits on activities, materials, and talk emphasize demonstrations, avoid distractions, minimize talk while work is in progress, then discuss and display work during the last 10 or 15 minutes of the session.
b. elicit thinking	emphasize open-ended tasks (without single, correct solutions known in advance), encourage exploratory learning.
c. reinforce learning	include kinetic as well as visual stimuli, provide time for quiet reflection, follow with verbal stimuli, introducing new words and encouraging each student to talk about his or her work.
2. to develop art skills	drawing, painting, and modeling clay.
3. to develop creative skills	emphasize individuality and originality.
4. to build self-confidence	emphasize reassurance and mutual respect; avoid situations that cause embarrassment, frustration or anxiety; never work on a student's paper or sculpture—offer suggestions on your own.
5. to set the stage for transfer	try to make the learning experience so rewarding that students will use what they learn for their own purposes in their own ways in other situations.
6. to assess ability and note changes	keep a log of observations; score, photograph or copy key works; date, number, and ask students to sign their work, leaving it with you until the end of the program.

First Session: Drawing from Imagination

MATERIALS: stimulus cards Groups A and C (people and things); paper 8½ × 11", pencils with erasers, and black, fine-line marking pens.

Objectives	Procedures
1. to develop ability to associate and form groups on the basis of class or function	
a. focus attention on associations	Cut the cards apart and present them in two adjacent groups, the two word cards surrounded by the appropriate drawings.
	Demonstrate the task by selecting the SD prince from one group and the SD ladder from the other, then quickly sketch the prince climbing the ladder to rescue a child from a burning house.
b. elicit associative thinking	Ask students to select one card from each group and draw a narrative picture: "Make your drawing tell a story about the picture ideas you choose. Show what is happening. Don't just copy these drawings. Change them or create your own. Draw other things, too, to make your story more interesting."
c. reinforce thinking	During the last 10 or 15 minutes, hold up the drawings one at a time. Point out their strengths and encourage each student to talk about his or her work and suggest a title. Write the titles along the bottom edges of the drawings.
	Ask students to return the cards to the groups they belong to when finished with them.
2. to develop expressiveness	Emphasize the content of drawings; emphasize their meanings rather than design or skill.
3 – 6	refer to page 112.
	Make xerox copies of first drawings to compare with later work.

Second Session: Drawing from Imagination

MATERIALS: same as in first session with the addition of felt-tipped markers, both thick and thin points, in various colors, 9 × 12" and 12 × 18" paper, and stimulus cards, Group B (animals).

Objectives	Procedures
1. to develop ability to associate and form groups on the basis of class or function	
a. focus attention	Present the stimulus cards in three adjacent groups, the word cards surrounded by the appropriate drawings.
b. elicit associative thinking	Ask students to select two cards from different groups and again draw narrative pictures using small or large sheets of paper as they wish. Also offer choices among the marker colors.
c. reinforce thinking	After drawings are finished, hold them up for approval and discussion, including titles.
	Mix the cards and ask students to sort them by category.
2. to develop expressiveness	Emphasize content rather than form.
3 – 6	Refer to page 112.

Third Session: Painting

MATERIALS: blue, red, and white poster paints, preferably in squeeze jar containers (or paper cups), 12 × 18" paper, palette knives (or flat wooden sticks), paper towels and sponges for cleaning up, newspapers for covering tables, smocks.

Objectives	Procedures
1. to develop ability to sequence	
a. focus attention on sequencing	Demonstrate mixing a series of blue tints by placing a dab of white on the upper right corner of a sheet of paper, and dab of blue on the upper left. With palette knife or stick, mix a series of tints between them from left to right by adding more and more white to tints of blue.

b. elicit thinking	Place dabs of blue and white on the upper left and right corners of students' papers and ask them to see how many tints of blue they can mix' between the two colors.
c. reinforce thinking	Encourage students to continue mixing or painting pictures on the rest of their paper: add more blue or white paint as needed on original dabs. As the paintings are finished, place them on the floor to dry, away from the painting area, and offer new sheets of paper.
	Limit second paintings to dabs of red on the upper left corner and white on the upper right corner, asking students to see how many tints of pink they can mix between them. They can then paint as they wish on the rest of their paper.
2. to develop skill in painting and sensitivity to nuances of color	Emphasize form rather than content and the colors, shapes, and designs rather than narrative meaning.
3 – 6	Refer to page 112.

Fourth Session: Painting

MATERIALS: yellow, blue, red, and white poster paints, 12 × 18 and 18 × 24 paper, 1" and pointed brushes, and other materials used in third session.

Objectives	**Procedures**
1. to develop ability to sequence	
a. focus attention on sequencing	Place a dab of yellow on the upper right corner of each student's paper (12 × 18), a dab of red on the upper left corner, and a dab of blue on the lower right corner.
b. elicit thinking	Ask students what they think will happen if they mix a series of colors between the dabs. Have them test their predictions by mixing the colors.

c. reinforce thinking	Encourage students to continue mixing and discovering colors, adding white to the lower left corner, replenishing colors as needed, and offering more paper for new paintings, either representational or abstract.
	Each time a student adds one color to another, he or she has created a sequence.
2. to develop sensitivity and skill	Emphasize both form and content.
3 – 6	Refer to page 112.

Fifth and Sixth Sessions: Painting from Imagination

MATERIALS: painting materials and stimulus cards, Group D (places)

Objectives	Procedures
1. to develop ability to form concepts of space, order, and class	
a. focus attention	Hold up one card at a time and ask, "Have you ever been to the beach? a farm? a volcano?" and so forth.
b. elicit thinking	Ask students to paint pictures about a visit to some interesting place. "Show something happening there, and be sure to include yourself."
c. reinforce thinking	In the time for discussion and display, point out horizontals, verticals, foregrounds and backgrounds. Encourage each student to talk about his or her painting and give it a title.
2. to develop art skills	Emphasize both form and content.
3 – 6	Refer to page 112.

Seventh Session: Predictive Drawing and Painting

MATERIALS: toy boats (made from the cork of a bottle with the mast being a toothpick, and the keel, a lump of clay) placed inside transparent jars filled with enough tinted water to float the boats; toy fishing lines (strings weighted with lumps of clay and suspended from sticks). There should be one boat, jar, and plumb-line for each 4 students; 8½ × 11 inch paper, pencils with erasers, and art materials of choice; a stool, chair, or pile of books so that boats can be presented at eye level on a horizontal surface.

Objectives	Procedures
1. to develop horizontal and vertical concepts	
a. focus attention on horizontality	Put the boat in the jar; half-fill with water and seal. Present the jar on its side at eye level on the table and ask, "How do you think the boat and water would look if we tilted the jar up at one end? Would they still look the same or would they look different?"
b. elicit thinking	Ask students to make a quick sketch.
c. focus attention on verticality	Present the fishing line against a door or other vertical object so that the parallel between them is visible. Ask, "How do you think the fishing line would look if we moved the pole up and down? Would it still look the same?"
d. elicit thinking	Ask students to turn over their papers and make a quick sketch of the fishing pole and line.
	Invite students to test out their predictions by manipulating the jars and lines. Be sure that the parallels (between table and water surface, door and plumbline), remain visible.
e. reinforce thinking	Ask students to draw or paint a picture of someone fishing on a lake.
	In the discussion and display, encourage comments from each student, use the words horizontal, vertical, and parallel but do not indicate that there is a correct or incorrect representation.

Eighth Session: Modeling Clay (Coils and Sonstroem Technique)*

MATERIALS: earth clay (or plasticene), modeling tools (or pencils, paper clips), 18 × 24″ oilcloth (or newspaper or cardboard), wire for cutting clay into lumps, plastic bags for storing sculpture. In advance, prepare a fist-sized lump of clay for each student and for yourself.

Objectives	Procedures
1. to develop concepts of space and ability to conserve	
a. focus attention	Give each student a lump of clay and ask him or her to hold it in both hands. With eyes closed, have them twist, pull out, and hollow it, then examine the shapes that were formed.
	Demonstrate rolling clay into "snakes" and balls.
b. elicit thinking	Ask students to divide their lumps of clay into two balls, and to make their balls the same by pinching clay from one and adding to the other.
	When they feel that the balls are the same, ask them to roll one into a snake, and ask if the ball and snake still have the same amounts of clay or if there is more in one than the other. Do not reveal correct answers.
c. reinforce (or reconsider) responses	Ask students to change their snakes back into balls, and with eyes closed and one ball in each hand, again compare their weights. Say, "if they are not the same, make them the same, and roll one ball into a snake." Again, ask them to judge the amounts and explain.
	Leave the remaining time free for modeling from imagination.
2. to develop art skills	Emphasize both form and content.
3 – 6	Refer to page 112.

*This conservation technique described in 1b was devised by A.M. Sonstroem (1966).

Ninth Session: Modeling Clay (Slab Technique)

MATERIALS: same as in sixth session with the addition of two flat sticks (about $12 \times 1 \times \frac{1}{4}$) and a wooden roller (about 12") for each student and yourself. These tools can be cut from old window shades.

Objectives	Procedures
1. to develop concepts of space and ability to conserve	
a. focus attention	Demonstrate how to form slabs by placing lumps of clay between parallel sticks and rolling them flat with both ends of the roller resting on the sticks. Slice off uneven edges, pressing them back onto the slab as needed and rolling again until the slab becomes a rectangle. Cut the rectangle into smaller rectangles and press pieces together, beginning to form a box. Demonstrate as quickly as possible, just long enough to convey the essential technique.
b. elicit thinking	Ask students to roll out slabs and put them together into three dimensional forms such boxes, banks, or houses.
c. reinforce thinking	Demonstrate, as needed, how to incise designs into slabs or add to the surface. Display and discuss finished work.
2. to develop skills in modeling and awareness of forms in space	Emphasize both form and content.
3 – 6	Refer to page 112.

Tenth Session: Modeling Clay (Brick Technique)

MATERIALS: same as in eighth and ninth sessions

Objectives	Procedures
1. to develop concepts of space, order, and class	
a. focus attention	Demonstrate building "bricks" by forming clay into small blocks and pressing them together. Use this process to start to build a human form beginning with feet, legs, and torso. Keep the demonstration brief.

b. elicit thinking	Ask students to build human, animal, or other forms by this method.
c. reinforce thinking	Ask students if they can put some of their sculptures together so that they convey meanings. Display, title, and discuss as in previous sessions.
2. to develop art skills	Emphasize both form and content.
3 – 6	Refer to page 112.

Eleventh Session: Drawing from Observation and Imagination

MATERIALS: an orange, a cylinder (made by rolling and taping a sheet of blue construction paper), paper 8 ½ × 11 inches, and art materials of choice.
There should be one set of objects for each four students

Objectives	Procedures
1. to develop awareness of spatial relationships (left-right, above-below, and front-back)	
a. focus attention	Place the objects on a sheet of paper either on a low table, surrounded by four desks and chairs, or in the center of a large table. Center the orange on one corner of the paper and the cylinder on the opposite corner. The arrangement should be below eye level so that the paper is seen as a plane rather than a line.
	Demonstrate drawing the arrangement from observation with a quick sketch (just long enough to convey the essential technique).
b. elicit thinking	Ask students to sketch the arrangement, including the paper base.
c. reinforce thinking	Ask students to change seats with a classmate on the opposite side of the arrangement and sketch it again. Call attention to the fact that the cylinder appears to the left of the orange from one point of view,

and to the right from another. Also call attention to the fact that the orange is in the foreground from one point of view, and in the background from another point of view.

d. to keep the emphasis open-ended

Limit the time spent drawing from observation to about ten minutes, then ask students to draw pictures about their families during the remainder of the session: "Show your house and the people who live there with you."

Twelfth Session: Drawing from Observation and Imagination

MATERIALS: one sculpture made by each student in a previous class and drawing materials of choice.

Objectives	Procedures
1. to develop concepts of space, order, and class	
a. focus attention	Ask each student to select one of his or her own sculptures to draw from observation.
b. elicit thinking	Ask them to make a quick sketch, then turn their sculptures around, and sketch again.
c. reinforce learning	Instead of pointing out mistakes, say, "Is this the way you want it to look?" If not, offer suggestions on scrap paper and leave final decsions to students.
d. to keep the emphasis open-ended	Limit the time for this drawing. Be guided by individual interests. Follow with free choice drawing.
2 – 6	Refer to page 112.

II

QUANTITATIVE
STUDIES

Atypical Children, Adolescents, and Adults

This chapter is concerned with studies of four atypical populations: Adolescents and adults in detention facilities; depressed children, adolescents, and adults in schools or hospitals; children with auditory or language impairments in special schools; and learning disabled students in special schools or specialized programs within typical schools. The studies incorporated the stimulus drawings into treatment plans, or used them to assess emotional states or cognitive skills.

☐ Adolescents and Adults in Detention Facilities

Identifying Self-Images in Response Drawings by Adolescents

The first part of this study explored three questions: 1) Do art therapists agree when identifying self-images in drawings by delinquent adolescents?; 2) Do social workers agree?; and 3) Can self-images be identified blindly, without knowing the person who drew them? (Silver & Ellison, 1995).

Method

JoAnne Ellison administered Form B of the DAS to 53 juveniles in a residential detention facility in California, and then discussed their drawings with them individually (Silver & Ellison, 1995). Of the 53 juveniles, 39 identified characters in their drawings as themselves. She placed their evaluations in a sealed envelope, made her own selections of self-images, then sent only the drawings to me for blind evaluation.

A psychologist then analyzed the levels of agreement among the two therapists and the 39 juveniles as an index of the validity of the Self-Image Measure.

The juveniles, ages 13–18, included all students attending four English classes in the detention facility. Most were from poor and working class families and incarcerated for the first time. Many had abused drugs and alcohol. Approximately 25% were special education students with specific learning disabilities. These students represented diverse ethnic backgrounds—African American, Mexican or Mexican American, Caucasian, Pacific Islander, Central American, Asian, and Native American.

In addition, three other art therapists and five social workers reviewed ten of the drawings, selected at random. These professionals judged blindly, identifiying the subjects they believed were self-images. Three of the five judges were registered art therapists (ATR); the other two had not yet received credentialing. Four of the social workers were credentialed professionals (MSW); one had not yet received credentialing.

Results

Ellison, who knew the students' histories and conducted the interviews, accurately matched 76.9% of the adolescents in identifying self-images. Silver, judging blindly, matched 71.8%. Approximately three out of four juveniles agreed with the art therapists (74.4%).

The interscorer agreement between Ellison and Silver, across the 53 respondents, was 94.3%. Five juveniles disagreed with both Ellison and Silver who agreed with each other in identifying their self-images. Their five drawings were reexamined.

One of the drawings is shown in Figure 9-1, a response by Roy, age 14, who had selected three stimulus drawings: the sulking person, the sword, and the couple with arms entwined. As he explained his drawing, "this man is very mad because a boy is going with his girlfriend, and the two couple don't know her boyfriend is watching, so he's going to grab the knife and kill both of them."

Asked how he imagined his characters would feel, he said the man was very angry, the girl and boy were happy, and, if he were in the picture, he would be the boy with the girl: "I'm the good guy. I couldn't kill nobody."

Both art therapists, however, identified the angry man as Roy's self-image. These agreements may reflect knowledge of art therapy codes, or an ability to recognize masked anger and anxiety about potential rivals.

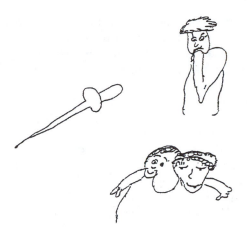

FIGURE 9-1. A drawing by Roy, age 14.

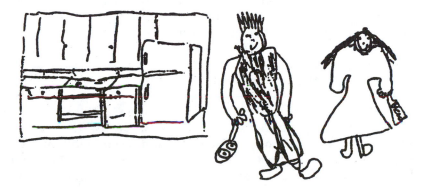

FIGURE 9-2. This is a Piture of my Mom and Dad in the Kitchen Cook me a Meal on a Sunday Morning, by Larry, age 13.

The average agreement among the five social workers was 54.0%; among the five art therapists, 78.2%; and among the subgroup of three registered art therapists, 93.4%.

Discussion

It was surprising to find that 54% of the social workers agreed on the identity of self-images, compared with approximately 93% of the registered art therapists.

Consider Figure 9-2, ... A Piture [sic] of my Mom and Dad ... by Larry who chose the king, queen, and kitchen environment. When Ellison asked if he had included himself in his drawing, he replied, "I'm in the other room at a table waiting for breakfast." The three registered art therapists agreed with Larry that he had omitted himself from his drawing. The seven other judges, identified the man, or both the man and woman, as Larry's self image.

How can differences in identifying self-images be explained? Answers may lie in the observation by Tinnen (1990) that the ability to perceive and interpret nonverbal messages in visual art forms is based on unconscious mimicry, which underlies emotions, aesthetic sensibility, and empathy, and belongs to the realm of primary process thinking. If art therapists are artists with psychological training, rather than mental health professionals with art training it seems more likely that they would use unconscious mimicry in perceiving and interpreting visual messages inaccessible to consciousness.

The findings suggest that discussion may not be essential for identifying self-images. Although discussion is preferable, and the more discussion, the more accurate interpretations are likely to be, the findings suggest that interviews can be bypassed, particularly in urgent situations, when circumstances, or time limitations, make interviews impossible.

The findings also raise questions about the training and skills required for assessing the content of drawings and suggest it would be useful to repeat this study with clearer instructions and larger samples of mental health professionals.

In the second part of this study (Silver & Ellison, 1995), Ellison presented case histories and discussed implications. She asked whether response drawings could provide quick, in-depth, economical, and valid knowledge about young male offenders, so that accurate and timely referrals and treatments could be made. She found very little resistance in responding to the DAS task, "it was like giving food to the starving" (Silver & Ellison, 1995, p. 154). The DAS seemed to circumvent the tendency to draw stereotypes.

Most of the drawings portrayed subjects as victims. Thirty juveniles drew fantasies of a man abandoned, often hoping for rescue—an image particularly evident in drawings completed shortly after arriving at the facility. These respondents also tended to draw isolated or aggressive, angry figures when newly incarcerated, and often depicted themselves as heroes defending the weak and warding off the enemy. Wish-fulfilling drawings about successful love relationships were also very common. There was an apparent sadness at missing girlfriends and fear that the girls would not be faithful. Of the eight identified alcoholic juveniles, four drew wish-fulfilling fantasies and four drew depressed, fearful, anxious, and sad figures. Clearly their drawings and writings concerned their current concerns or wishes.

Originally, Ellison had hoped that aggressive or acting out individuals could be differentiated from those who were depressed or acting-in, but found that many, although depressed, were able to avoid their feelings by acting out when not incarcerated. In the structured setting of the probation camp, with highly imposed controls, they became more sad, anxious, and fearful, and demonstrated more self-destructive behavior. One juvenile, whose responses concerned hopeless, sad themes, committed suicide shortly after his release. From reviewing his responses, Ellison observed that both sad and aggressive stories may indicate depression, and that happy fantasies may indicate denial by equally depressed youths who may be more resistant to treatment.

Ellison concluded that a structured art assessment, such as the DAS, could be useful in evaluating juveniles with conduct disorders. She noted that teachers could present the DAS in group settings and have the drawings evaluated later by an art therapist, even if the therapist is unable to speak directly to the respondents. She also observed that the tendency to draw same-gender subjects found in previous studies was again confirmed, supporting the assumption that the self tends to be the subject of projective drawings. She also noted that Hispanic males have an affinity for drawing and that translating the DAS into Spanish might be worthwhile.

Gender Differences in the Fantasies of Delinquent and Nondelinquent Adolescents

Building on the previous study, 138 adolescents, ages 13–17, were asked to respond to the DAS task (Silver, 1996a). They included 53 boys and 11 girls, wards of a juvenile court, committed to a residential treatment facility for adolescents in California. They included all students who were attending four English classes in the facility and responded to the DAS stimulus drawings presented in their classroom by a registered art therapist.

The control subjects included nondelinquent, presumably normal adolescents, 29 boys and 45 girls, attending four schools in Ohio, Florida, and New York. These students were attending English or other classes in their schools and responded to the DAS subtest which was presented by classroom teachers or by registered art therapists.

Method

The responses were divided by gender and delinquency into drawings about solitary subjects and drawings about relationships, then evaluated on a 5-point rating scale based on attitudes toward the self-images or relationships portrayed. Mean scores were also analyzed and compared.

Results

The first analysis evaluated whether gender or delinquency were related to self-images scores on the rating scale. Using a 2×2 ANOVA, no significant results were obtained (the male mean score was 2.52, the female mean score, 2.92).

The second analysis examined whether the proportions of drawings about solitary subjects or assaultive relationships differed depending on delinquency or gender. Overall, boys and girls differed on both assaultive (Chi square $(1) = 11.00$, $p < .01$) and solitary content (Chi-square $(1) = 6.33$, $p < .05$); 31.7% of the boys drew pictures about assaultive relationships as compared with 5.4% of the girls. The effect was reversed for solitary content: 37.5% of the girls drew pictures about solitary subjects as compared with 15.9% of the boys.

Solitary content also distinguished between delinquent and control groups: 33.8% of the control respondents drew solitary subjects as compared with 14.1% of the delinquent respondents.

In drawings about assaultive relationships by the control subjects, gender difference reached significance (Chi-square $(1) = 9.11$, $p < .01$), but the gender difference in drawings by the delinquent subjects did not reach significance. Although 28.3% of the delinquent boys drew assaultive relationships, no delinquent girls drew assaultive relationships. Aggressive humor was found in 45.4% of the drawings about assaults by control group boys, but not found in any other group.

In drawings about sad or helpless solitary subjects, the gender differences were again large in the control group but small in the delinquent group. When *negative* attitudes toward solitary subjects were examined, proportionally more girls than boys in both groups drew sad or helpless subjects (delinquent girls, 18.1%, control girls, 17.8%, delinquent boys, 9.4%, control boys, 6.9%). When *positive* attitudes were examined, the control group predominated (control girls, 20%, control boys, 13.8%, delinquent boys, 3.7%, delinquent girls, 0). Greater gender differences were found among presumably normal adolescents than among delinquent adolescents.

Discussion

When mean scores were examined, no differences in gender or delinquency were found. Differences appeared, however, when drawings about assaultive relationships or solitary subjects were examined more closely.

It was surprising to find that proportionally more nondelinquent than delinquent boys drew assaultive relationships. Perhaps the finding can be explained by the difference between fantasizing about violence and acting violently. A boy who has internalized prohibitions against acting out biological drives, may fantasize more than one who acts out. It also may be that incarceration for antisocial behavior inhibits expressing aggressive fantasies.

Although most drawings about assaultive relationships seemed to express wish-fulfilling fantasies, others seemed to express conflict or denial. Among the delinquent boys who drew such fantasies, 47% seemed to feel a need to justify the violence they expressed, such as killing bad guys to protect innocent victims. A similar proportion of nondelinquent boys who drew assaultive fantasies used aggressive humor (see Figure 7-1), Godzilla Vs Mighty Mouse) perhaps as a form of defense or denial.

In drawings about solitary subjects, fantasies about successful self-images appeared more often in drawings by nondelinquent girls than nondelinquent boys, but no delinquent girls drew successful solitary self-images, or even expressed positive feelings toward solitary subjects. The finding that approximately 18% of both delinquent and nondelinquent girls expressed negative feelings toward self-image solitary subjects concurs with the findings of other investigators, cited earlier, that adolescence seems to be a particularly difficult time for some girls. The finding that none of the delinquent girls expressed positive feelings toward the solitary subjects they portrayed suggests that they may be more at risk, or that incarceration dims or extinguishes wish-fulfilling fantasies.

Comparing Adolescent Sex Offenders with Nonoffending Adolescents

Brandt (1995) administered the Draw a Story and Stimulus Drawings tasks to 14 male adolescent sex offenders who had been incarcerated in a residential facility. Their ages ranged from 12–18, averaging 16 years of age. She compared their emotional content scores, their use of space, and use of detail with the scores of nonoffending adolescents and depressed adolescents. Brandt was also concerned with the importance of visual arts in treating and assessing the offenders.

Method

At their first meeting, Brant administered DAS Forms A and B to the group of offenders. At their second meeting, she administered the Stimulus Drawing assessment, and at their third meeting, asked them to complete self-reports.

In a study of interrater reliability, and to compare the mean scores of offenders with the scores of nonoffending adolescents and depressed adolescents, the response drawings were evaluated by two judges. Recurrent images were also examined.

Results

The correlation coefficients of the judges' scores averaged .72. The mean score of the sex offenders on both assessments (1.89) was significantly lower (more negative) than the mean scores of the nonoffending male adolescents (2.73) as well as the depressed male adolescents (3.14) who were assumed to be nonoffenders. No significant difference was found in the use of space or detail.

Recurrent images included nine responses to the king and prince stimulus drawings, seven to the snake, five to the knife, and four to angry persons (three to the standing angry person with arm raised, one to the seated angry person) stimulus drawings. The offenders tended to present themselves as powerful, angry, and superior, fighting aggressively in hostile environments.

Discussion

The findings suggested that sex offenders are likely to be depressed and likely to perceive themselves and their worlds in strongly negative ways. The findings also suggested that studio art experience can enable art therapists and others who work with sex offenders to tap into emotionality, and therefore can be useful in treatment programs, which remain primarily cognitive and behavioral.

A Study of Offender/Patients in a Maximum Security Psychiatric Prison

Janis Woodall, ATR-BC, and Megan Van Meter, ATR-BC, are using the SDT Drawing from Imagination subtest to determine group placement and art therapy treatment needs for male offender/patients. Additionally, these art therapists are in the beginning stages of comparing subtest results to high-risk behavior indicators, such as suicidal gestures that require medical attention, assaults toward staff and other offenders, formal disciplinary actions imposed, and the results of several evaluations administered by the prison's psychology department.

Woodall and Van Meter will use correlational studies to determine whether their findings support the use of the Drawing from Imagination subtest to identify high risk offender/patients before they have an opportunity to endanger themselves or others.

A Study of Children at Risk for Delinquency

Marcy Purdy, ATR-BC, is engaged in a study designed to enhance the lives of children considered at risk, by providing art programs that raise their self-esteem, and encourage them to become productive citizens. The study, supported by a government grant, is using the SDT Drawing from Imagination subtest to assess results.

Thirty-one children, ages 6–13, who met one of two criteria—living with a single parent or guardian, or enrolled in any special program—were selected. They attended a two-week summer arts camp where they were free to choose from a variety of activities including music, movement, drama, and several visual arts. The SDT was administered before and after the program. From this information, six students received scholarships to work individually with a particular artist for the remainder of the school year.

The camp will be offered again next summer. Investigators will correlate test scores to determine the relationship of art experiences to the self-esteem of the participants.

☐ Clinically Depressed Children, Adolescents, and Adults

Three studies examined the hypothesis that strongly negative responses to the stimulus drawing task are associated with clinical depression, and that the task can be used as a screening technique in schools to identify students with masked depression or elsewhere for early identification of individuals who may be at risk for depression. The studies were described briefly in the introduction to Draw A Story in Chapter 2, and will be discussed more fully here.

Screening 254 Children and Adolescents for Depression

The first study had noted an urgent need to identify children or adolescents who may be depressed or at risk for suicide, and theorized that stimulus drawings might be used for the early detection of depressive illness (Silver, 1988a). It also was noted that drawings tend to be less guarded than speech and offer glimpses into the ways we see ourselves and our worlds. In four studies (Silver, 1987) involving more than 600 children and adolescents, a few fantasies about committing suicide as well as more than a few fantasies about death, dying, or hopeless situations had appeared unexpectedly in responses to the Drawing from Imagination task (Fig. 3-7 was an example).

The study asked two questions: Are strongly negative responses linked to clinical depression? And do negative responses tend to be temporary or do they persist over periods of time?

Method

Between October, 1986 and April, 1987 19 art therapists, school counselors, and teachers presented the Form A Draw a Story task to 254 children and adolescents in public schools, special schools, and hospitals. The students ranged in age from 8–21, and resided in Arizona, Pennsylvania, Montana, New Jersey, New York, and Oregon. One hundred eleven subjects were presumably normal, 27 were clinically depressed, 61 were emotionally disturbed with nondepressive psychopathology, 31 were learning disabled, and 24 were normal children who responded to the drawing task on two occasions.

Results

Approximately 56% of the clinically depressed students responded with strongly negative fantasies compared with 11% of the normal students, 21% of the emotionally disturbed nondepressed students, and 32% of the learning disabled students.

To determine whether these differences were significant, the chi-square test was used. The proportion of depressed students with strongly negative fantasies was greater than the proportion of normal subjects with strongly negative fantasies (chi-square, 27.63, $p < .001$). The proportion of depressed subjects with strongly negative fantasies was also significantly greater than the proportion of emotionally disturbed subjects with strongly negative fantasies but to a lesser degree (chi-square, 10.54, $p < .01$). The proportion of depressed subjects with strongly negative fantasies was not significantly greater than the proportion of learning disabled subjects with strongly negative fantasies (chi-square 3.269, $p < .05$).

To determine whether the negativity of responses reflected temporary moods, 24 third graders were presented with the drawing task on two occasions. When 12 presumably normal children who had previously responded with strongly or moderately negative fantasies were retested after an interval of approximately one month, seven received the same scores, three had higher scores and two had lower scores. Subsequently, when 12 other children were retested after an interval of approximately two years, 11 received the same scores.

Discussion

Based on these findings, there appeared to be a link between depressive illness and strongly negative responses to the Draw a Story task. Although strongly negative responses did not necessarily indicate depression, and conversely, positive responses did not exclude depression, the findings seemed to indicate that a child or adolescent who receives the lowest score may be at risk for depression. A second observation was that the children who were retested demonstrated that negative responses seem to persist over time, suggesting that these scores reflect characteristic attitudes rather than passing moods. A third observation noted that a comparably large proportion of learning-disabled students received the lowest score and no significant difference emerged between their scores and the scores of patients diagnosed as clinically depressed.

Screening 350 Children, Adolescents, and Adults for Depression

This study built on the previous study by adding adults and expanding the sample populations to a total of 350 respondents (Silver, 1988b). Five additional art therapists volunteered to present Form A to the patients or students with whom they worked. The respondents included 35 clinically depressed children or adolescents, 15 clinically depressed adults, 74 emotionally disturbed children or adolescents with nondepressive psychopathlogy, 64 learning disabled adolescents, 18 hearing impaired children and adolescents, 27 senior adults, and 117 presumably normal children and adolescents, ages 5 through 19, residing in two additional states, Illinois and Georgia as shown in Fig. 2-19. Approximately 63% of the depressed children and adolescents responded with strong negative fantasies, compared with 11.9% of normal students, 19% emotionally disturbed, 30% of the learning disabled, and 30% of the adults.

Results

A chi square analysis indicated that the proportion of depressed children and adolescents scoring lowest was significantly greater than the proportion of any other group scoring lowest: Compared with the normal group, the chi-square was 43.2, $p < .0005$; with the emotionally disturbed group, the chi-square was 20.6, $p < .0005$; with the learning disabled group, 11.1, $p < .001$; with the hearing-impaired group, 19.5, $p < .0005$; with

TABLE 9-1. Analysis of differences in proportion of strongly negative responses among depressed, normal, emotionally disturbed, learning disabled and deaf children, adolescents, and adults.

	Depressed Children & Adolescents	Normal	Emotionally Disturbed	Learning Disabled	Deaf	Elderly	Depressed Adults
1 point	22	12	14	19	0	2	2
2 or more points	13	105	83	45	18	25	13
x^2		43.2	20.6	11.1	19.5	20.0	10.4
p		<.0005	<.0005	<.001	<.0005	<.0005	>.005

the elderly group, 20.0, $p < .0005$; and with the depressed adults, 10.4, $p > .005$, as shown in Table 9-1.

Only 2 of the 15 clinically depressed adults, however, received the lowest score whereas 9 scored higher (2 subjects were ambivalent, 3 were ambiguous, and 4 were unemotional).

Discussion

These findings suggested that strongly negative responses, characterized by the lowest score (1 point), are associated with adolescent or childhood depression, and that the DAS instrument might be useful as a first step in identifying some, but not all, depressed children and adolescents.

Although most of the findings in this study supported the first study, differences emerged in the sample of learning disabled adolescents. Unlike the first study, significant difference was found between the scores of this larger learning disabled sample and the scores of depressed adolescents ($p = <.001$).

This finding about adults raised several questions. Did it reflect conflict or denial?; Were the adults more reticent or guarded?; and, Does the DAS task have little value in revealing depression among adults? These questions prompted the following study.

Comparing Self-Reports, the Amount of Detail, and the Use of Space, in Responses by Depressed and Nondepressed Adolescents and Adults

A third study of depressed respondents asked whether self-reports or the uses of space and detail, provided evidence of clinical depression, as has been suggested by other investigators (Silver, 1993a).

TABLE 9-2. Rating scales for assessing the use of space, the use of detail, and the self-report.

Use of space
   1 point: less than 1/4 of the area is covered by the drawing
   2 points: less than 1/3 of the area
   3 points: approximately 1/2 of the area
   4 points: approximately 2/3 of the area
   5 points: entire drawing area

Use of detail
   1 point: copying or stick figures, no added detail
   2 points: few new details or changes
   3 points: moderate amount of details are added
   4 points: many details, moderately original or expressive
   5 points: many details, highly original and expressive

Self-report
   1 point: sad or very unhappy
   2 points: angry, frightened, or unhappy
   3 points: response is unclear
   4 points: o.k. or happy
   5 points: very happy

Method

In addition to the Emotional Content scale, a second scale was devised to assess the responses of 107 depressed and nondepressed adults and adolescents. The scale included a self-report and assessed the use of space and detail, as shown in Table 9-2.

The respondents included 47 hospitalized patients previously diagnosed as clinically depressed, including 18 women and girls, ages 12–69, and 23 men, ages 17–53. The nondepressed respondents included 34 women, ages 19–72, and 26 men, ages 20–77.

Results

No significant differences were found between depressed and nondepressed respondents in the use of space or detail. Gender differences, however, emerged: Female drawings ($m = 1.84$) showed significantly fewer details than male drawings ($m = 2.31$) (F (1,103) = 4.27, $p < .05$).

Self-reports tended to be inconsistent with Emotional Content scores. Many respondents, hospitalized for major depression, indicated that they felt "o.k" or "very happy," although some negative self-reports accompanied negative themes.

In Emotional Content, the depressed men tended to respond with negative themes whereas the depressed women tended to respond with neutral themes. The groups of nondepressed men and women did not differ significantly.

The depressed men had more negative themes than the nondepressed men (Chi square (1,2) = 4.96, $p < 0$, borderline significance. The depressed women tended to draw ambivalent or ambiguous fantasies (few drew pictures with unemotional themes). It was not clear, however, whether their neutral responses were associated with depression.

Discussion

Denial, reticence, or the effects of anti-depressant medication may have affected these responses. It may also be that responding to this brief self-report in the presence of others discouraged thoughtful or sincere responses.

These three studies support the hypothesis that strongly negative responses to the Draw a Story task are associated with clinical depression among children and adolescents. The correlations found between responses to Draw a Story and the SD Drawing from Imagination subtest seem to indicate that both assessments can be used to screen for depression among children and adolescents, and possibly among men. Their value in screening women for depression remains unclear. It is hoped that further study of larger populations will clarify whether ambivalent or ambiguous responses by women are associated with masked depression.

☐ Children with Auditory and Language Impairments

Originally, the stimulus drawing tasks were designed to communicate with students in schools for deaf children. Subsequently, the tasks were used in three studies that compared these children with unimpaired children, and in each study, the performances of children with communication disorders equaled or excelled the performances of unimpaired children, either before or after experimental art programs (Silver, 1996b). The studies are summarized below.

Cognitive Skills Development Through Art Experiences

In the first study, a project supported by a State Urban Education grant, I worked with a group of 34 children who had communication disorders (Silver, 1973, 1975a). They included Burt, Vi, and Charlie, whose histories are presented in Chapter 6. My first goal was to help the children develop concepts of space, sequential order, and class inclusion, without neglecting aesthetic and creative growth, as discussed previously. To compare the cognitive skills of these children with the skills of children with no known disorders, the tasks were administered once to 68 children in a suburban public school.

Method

The experimental group consisted of a randomly selected 50% sample of 12 classes in a special school for children with communication disorders. The remaining 34 children served as a control group. The art program was provided once a week for 11 weeks in the fall and 9 weeks in the spring. To determine the art programs effectiveness, the children responded to drawing tasks before and after the program.

In addition, two judges, a university professor of art and a painter who was also a registered art therapist, were asked to evaluate three drawings or paintings produced by each child in the Fall experimental group ($n = 18$)—the child's first drawing, last drawing, and a drawing produced at midterm. The 54 drawings were identified only by number and shown in random order to conceal the sequence in which they were produced. The judges, working independently, rated each work for art skills and ability to represent thoughts and feelings, objects, and events. They used a rating scale that ranged from low to high levels of art skills and sensitivity to art values.

Results

In Drawing from Imagination, the experimental group improved in the combined abilities of selecting, combining, and representing at the $p < .01$ level of significance. The scores of the normal children were superior when compared to the impaired children's pretest but not significantly better than the impaired childrens' posttests as shown in Figure 9-3. The impaired children's pretest mean score was 8.0; their posttest mean was 11.47; $t = 3.62$, significant at the $p < .01$ level with $df = 33$ (two-tailed test). Their scores were also significantly higher than the scores of the control group at the .01 level. The posttest mean score of the control group was 8.44.

In Drawing from Observation, the experimental group improved significantly at the $p < .05$ level. The control group did not improve, as shown in Figure 9-4. Although the normal children had higher scores on the pretest, and the impaired experimental children had higher scores on the posttest, there was no significant difference between the groups. The pretest mean of the experimental group was 9.37; their posttest mean, 11.43, $t = 3.03$,

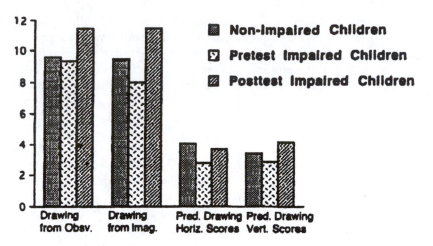

FIGURE 9-3. Comparing pretest and posttest scores of language/hearing impaired, control, and unimpaired children.

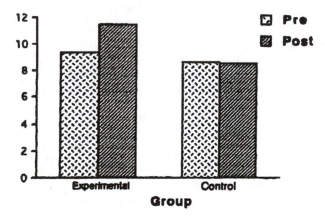

FIGURE 9-4. Comparing pretest and posttest scores of language/hearing impaired experimental and control groups.

significant at the $p < .05$ level with df $= 15$ (two-tailed test). The pretest mean of the control group was 8.56; posttest mean, 8.50. The mean for the unimpaired children was 9.63 ($t = .5877$).

In Predictive Drawing, the experimental group again improved significantly at the $p < .01$ level. The control group did not improve. Comparing impaired and unimpaired children, the normal children had significantly higher scores on the pretest in both horizontal and vertical orientation. After the art program, no significant difference was found in horizontal orientation. In vertical orientation however, the impaired experimental group was significantly superior to the unimpaired group.

In art skills and sensitivity to art values, the gains were significant at the $p < .01$ level of probability. As rated by the painter-art therapist, the mean score of drawings produced in the first class was 4.44; the mean score in the last class, 7.27, $t = 3.13$, gains significant at the $p < .01$ level. As rated by the art professor who also scored blindly, the mean score of the first class was 3.66; the last class, 6.33; $t = 3.29$, also significant at the $p < .01$ level.

The developmental art procedures used in this project, and subsequent studies, are described in Chapter 8. Additional data is presented in the SDT manual (Silver, 1996a).

Comparing SDT Scores of Hearing and Hearing-Impaired Girls and Boys

In a subsequent study (Silver, 1996a), responses to the SDT tasks by 27 hearing impaired children (some with multiple handicaps), were compared with the scores of 28 hearing children matched in age (ages 9–11) and selected at random (Silver, 1996a).

Method

Subjects included 13 girls and 14 boys in an urban, nonresidential school for hearing impaired children. The subjects were in the fourth grade and had responded to the SDT as part of the National Institute of Education Project discussed later in this chapter. As measured by the WISC assessment, their IQs ranged from 72 to 130. One of the boys also had language disabilities; one girl and one boy had multiple disabilities.

The hearing subjects included 14 girls and 14 boys who were matched in age and selected at random from responses to the SDT administered in two schools by a classroom teacher in New Jersey and an art therapist in Pennsylvania.

Results

In Drawing from Observation, no significant gender differences or differences between hearing and hearing impaired children emerged. In Predictive Drawing, the hearing impaired children received significantly higher scores than the hearing children in vertical orientation (F(1,51) = 14.34, $p < .001$). No significant differences were found in horizontal orientation or in ability to sequence. The mean scores were 3.13 hearing impaired and 2.00 hearing impaired, respectively as shown in Figure 9-5.

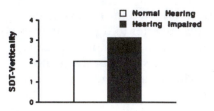

FIGURE 9-5. Comparing scores of deaf and hearing children in ability to predict and represent vertically.

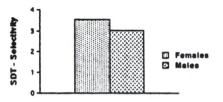

FIGURE 9-6. Comparing scores of girls and boys in ability to select.

In Drawing from Imagination, the girls received higher scores than the boys in ability to select to a degree significant at the .05 level ($F(1,51) = 5.49$, $p < .05$). No other gender differences emerged. This finding is shown in Figure 9-6.

The hearing children received significantly higher scores in all sub-tests: ability to select ($F(1,51) = 12.85$, $p < .001$), ability to combine ($F(1,51) = 57.66$, $p < .000001$), and ability to represent ($F(1,51) = 30.99$, $p < .000001$). The means were 3.68 vs. 2.90 for selecting, 3.93 vs. 1.98 for combining, and 3.89 vs. 2.27 for representing, as shown in Figure 9-7.

Discussion

It was unexpected to find the hearing impaired children superior to the hearing children in vertical orientation. Only 4 of the 55 children drew vertical houses, and three of the four were deaf. Apparently, they had learned that houses remain vertical when cantilevered or supported by posts. No significant differences were found in the four remaining spatial abilities.

In Drawing from Imagination, the hearing impaired children had significantly lower scores than the hearing children. Perhaps these mental operations cannot be separated from language skills, or the hearing impaired children had less experience in selecting, combining, and representing due to language deficiencies. If so, additional experiences in drawing from imagination might lead to gains that transfer to language skills.

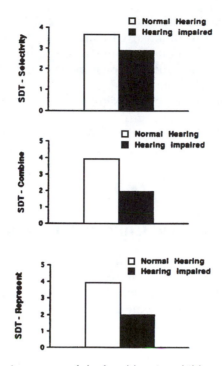

FIGURE 9-7. Comparing scores of deaf and hearing children and ability to select, ability to combine, and ability to represent.

Because of the many reports of male superiority in performing the Piagetian task of liquid horizontality, it was surprising to find that girls received significantly higher scores than boys in Ability to Select, and that no significant gender differences emerged in spatial abilities. Further study with larger populations may provide explanations.

The findings of this study support the theory that the SDT can be effective in assessing gender differences and similarities in cognitive skills as well as the cognitive strengths and weaknesses that may be characteristic of hearing impaired children.

Comparing SDT Scores of Deaf, Learning Disabled, and Unimpaired Girls and Boys

This study expanded the previous study by adding a sample of 28 learning-disabled children (Silver, 1996a). The data were analyzed by using ANOVA and LSD tests to determine which groups differed on which measures.

In vertical orientation, the deaf children had higher scores than either the learning disabled or unimpaired children at the .05 level of probability. The unimpaired and deaf groups received higher scores than the learning disabled in left-right relationships (as might be expected with reading difficulties). The unimpaired groups scored highest in ability to select, combine, and represent. No significant differences were found in sequencing, horizontality, or depth.

These findings amplify the evidence found in the previous study and support the theory that the SDT can be effective in assessing the cognitive strengths and weaknesses of hearing impaired, learning disabled, and unimpaired girls and boys.

☐ Learning Disabled Children and Adolescents

Since the stimulus drawings procedures had proved useful with children who had auditory and language impairments, I wondered if they would be useful with children who had an opposite constellation of skills—verbal strengths and visual-motor weaknesses, and whether the procedures could be used effectively by other art therapists.

Developing and Evaluating Cognitive Skills

In the first study, 11 graduate students who had registered for an elective course in art therapy, worked under supervision with 11 unselected learning impaired children (Silver & Lavin, 1977). They used the art procedures developed in the State Urban Education Project. After 10 weekly one hour periods, the children showed significant gains in concepts of space, order, and class inclusion, as measured by the stimulus drawing tasks.

Method

The children were not systematically selected. Announcements were sent to newspapers and to a learning disabilities association, stating that art classes were being offered. Children were enrolled as their applications were received. All but two had disabilities of a visual-spatial-motor nature, and these two were eliminated from the statistical analysis.

The children attended ten weekly one hour classes on Saturday mornings, working together in a large studio under the supervision of the instructor who had developed the procedures. The graduate students attended three preliminary lectures. Thereafter, each week, half an hour before the children arrived, they prepared for the day's activities. They stayed for half hour after the children left to organize their notes and evaluate results.

When the classes ended, six graduate students scored the 44 pre- and posttest drawings, identified only by number and presented in random order. The results were analyzed for scorer reliability and for changes in Drawing from Imagination, Predictive Drawing, and Drawing from Observation.

An analysis of variance was used to determine the reliability of measurements. The effectiveness of the training program was evaluated by using a t-test ($N = 11$) for correlated means to determine the significance of differences in mean pre- and posttest scores. Separate analyses were performed for scores on the ability to form groups, spatial orientation, and other abilities.

Results

In ability to form groups, the obtained reliability coefficent was .825; in spatial orientation, the reliability coefficent was .944, indicating that the six judges had a similar frame of reference and displayed a high degree of agreement in scoring the tests.

In evaluating the effectiveness of the program, all the obtained t-values were statistically significant. The improvement in ability to form groups ($t = 4.79$) and in ordering a matrix ($t = 6.54$) was significant at the .01 level. Improvement in spatial orientation was significant at the .05 level ($t = 2.42$). Thus the learning impaired children in the art program improved significantly in the three areas of cognitive development under consideration.

Discussion

The findings supported the hypothesis that children with learning disabilities would show improvement in the three cognitive areas when taught by graduate students using the art procedures developed in the project for children with communication disorders.

The following year, another group of graduate students worked with a group of children selected by school administrators for performing below grade level academically. These children also made significant gains at the $p < .01$ level in Drawing from Imagination, and at the $p < .05$ level in both Predictive Drawing and Drawing from Observation (Silver, 1982a). The success of these programs seems to indicate that art therapy procedures can be used to assist learning disabled children in expressing concepts nonverbally through visual-motor channels.

The National Institute of Education Project

This project built upon the previous studies, attempting to verify their findings with a wider variety of settings and a more diverse population (Silver, Lavin, Boeve, Hayes, Itzler, O'Brien, Wohlberg, & Terner, 1980). In addition to the art therapy program, the project examined the relationship of the SDT to traditional measures of intelligence or achievement.

Method

Five graduate students worked in five urban and suburban schools with 84 children, ages 7–11. School administrators had selected the children because they were performing at least one year below grade level. The schools included a special school for learning disabled children, and four schools for typical students as well as those with special needs. From this population, experimental and matched control groups were selected based on their SDT scores.

As originally planned, only children who scored at least 3 points in Drawing from Imagination would participate, but in order to include a sufficient number of children in each school, it was necessary to include many children with lower scores. A matched control group received no such special treatment.

Each of the graduate students worked with two groups of five children for approximately 40 minutes a week for 12 weeks. During the first 6-week period, all groups used the same procedures. During the second 6-weeks the graduate students adapted the procedures to meet the needs of individuals students and devised procedures of their own. They also administered the SDT to experimental and control groups before and after the art program.

Results

The posttest scores of the experimental group showed significant gains over the pretest scores, but no significant differences were found between the posttest scores of experimental and control groups. A school-by-school analysis showed significant differences between pretest and posttest scores in one school only, the school for learning disabled children. In this school, the posttest scores of the experimental group were significantly higher than posttest scores of the control group.

Discussion

It is not clear why the art program in the school for children with learning disabilities was more effective than in the other schools, or why the gains found in previous studies failed to materialize in the other four schools. It may be that the finding reflects superior skills of one art therapist, or too much flexibility in the procedures used. By specifying procedures for only 6 of the 12 periods, too many variables may have been introduced. On the other hand, the finding may reflect distinctions between learning disabled students and students who perform at least one year below grade level in reading or mathematics.

Four Masters' Theses

These studies used the SDT as a pretest posttest measure to assess the experimental programs they provided for learning-disabled children. The theses by Moser (1980) and Hayes (1978) were discussed in Chapter 2.

Anna Hiscox (1990) hypothesized that learning disabled students would fall within the normal range on IQ tests that were not based on verbal language. She administered the California Achievement Test (CAT) and the SDT to 14 learning disabled, 14 reading disabled, and 14 unimpaired children in the third, fourth, and fifth grades in California. The results supported her hypothesis. On both tests, the unimpaired children had the highest mean scores. The learning disabled group had higher mean scores than the reading disabled group who performed within the middle range of both groups. The difference in the mean and standard deviation between groups validated the rejection of the null hypothesis at the .05 level of significance.

Karen Henn (1990) examined whether an integrated approach to teaching can have a significant effect on the understanding of horizontal, vertical, and depth relationships by multiple handicapped students in New York. Her subjects included 24 students, ages 16–21, some of whom were nonverbal. She used the SDT Drawing from Observation subtest as a pre-posttest measure. Her program included a movement activity accompanied by music, a visual art activity, and a closing activity. In assessing interscorer reliability, Henn found correlations of .95 for horizontal relationships, .86 for vertical relationships, and .84 for relationships in depth. A correlation of .92 was found for combined gains on the three variables. The posttest scores for all three criteria were significantly higher than the pretest scores ($t = -2.96$, $p = < .0058$).

Linda Blasdel (1997) assessed the impact of creative art experiences on the critical thinking skills of inner city students in the fifth grade in Kansas. She hypothesized that experiential learning through the manipulation of art materials builds high-order thinking, allowing a synthesis of knowledge with critical thinking skills, defined as logical analysis and creative construction that leads to effective problem-solving. She administered the SDT Predictive Drawing and Drawing from Imagination subtests together with the Cornell Critical Thinking Test, as pre- and posttests to experimental and control groups. Although significant differences between pretest and posttest scores were not achieved, the results suggested that extending the art experiences could yield evidence to support the value of art experiences in building critical thinking skills.

Susan Marshall (1998) used a developmental program to enhance the cognitive skills of two groups of learning disabled children in Maine. The program included painting, Drawing from Observation, Drawing from Imagination, and imagination games. She administered the SDT and a second measure consisting of ten conservation tasks before and after the program to determine whether abilities improved. Group A included five children ages 7–10 who attended 14 sessions. Group B included four children ages 13 and 14 who attended 9 sessions. The young children in Group A showed increases in mean total scores from 16.46 to 21.09, gaining in each of the subtests. The most marked and consistent gain was in Drawing from Imagination. The adolescents in group B showed little gain, their total mean scores increasing from 25.50 to 26.0.

10

Age, Gender, and Cultural Differences Among Typical Children, Adolescents, and Adults

This chapter summarizes findings of age and gender differences among respondents with no known disabilities. The studies included here look at attitudes, emotions, spatial skills, and cultural differences among children, adolescents, and adults in Brazil and Australia.

When a group of 102 adults at a professional conference responded to the Drawing from Imagination task, the question of whether young women draw more negative fantasies than other groups arose. Most respondents drew pictures about unhappy people in unpleasant situations, and most were young women. Was this typical, or did this group have unusually negative associations? In search of answers, the Drawing from Imagination task was presented to various groups of men, women, girls, and boys.

☐ Background

It is useful to begin by reviewing the gender differences observed by several investigators. Leonard Schlain (1998) writes that emotionally, males and females respond differently to the same stimuli. They have different perceptions of the world, and different ways of knowing: these differences

developed from the male role of hunter/killer and the female role of gath-
erer/nurturer. To accommodate these differences, nature redesigned the
human brain, eye, and hand. Males gained attributes that are desirable
for hunters, such as the ability to remain emotionless and focus on single tasks, just as females gained attributes desirable for nurturers, such
as understanding the needs of offspring and performing multiple tasks
simultaneously. Women tend to be more aware of emotions than men.

Gilligan and her associates (1988) examined moral judgments and found
gender differences. The feminine mode is based on concepts of care and
responsibility to others; the masculine mode, on concepts of detachment
and self-sufficiency. According to Tannen (1990), males tend to focus on
independence and status; females, on relationships. Are the differences
observed in verbal expressions, evident in drawings? Five studies have
explored gender and age differences in the attitudes and emotions expressed in response to the Drawing from Imagination task (Silver, 1987a;
Silver, 1992; Silver, 1993b; Silver, 1997; Silver, 1998a).

☐ Age and Gender Differences in Attitudes toward Principal Subjects and Environments

The first study asked if there were measurable differences in the positive or
negative attitudes expressed through drawings (Silver, 1987a, 2000a). The
task was presented to males and females ($N = 326$) in four groups: third
graders, high school seniors, young adults, and senior adults. Responses
were rated on a scale ranging from strongly negative to strongly positive
fantasies about the subjects and environments portrayed. For each drawing, two scores were obtained: one for the Principal Subject, one for the
Environment.

Significant differences were found between males and females across
all age groups, as measured by a $2 \times 4 \times 2$ Factorial Analysis of Variance. Males consistently portrayed more negative surroundings inhabited
by more positively seen subjects to a degree exceeding the .05 level of
probability.

These findings were supported by a Newman-Keuls Multiple Range Test
which found that males gave higher ratings to principal subjects than to
environments, while females showed no significant differences. Female
ratings correlated significantly in each age group, that is, as their ratings for
Principal Subject increased, their rating for Environment also increased.
Both males and females portrayed subjects more positively than they portrayed environments, also to significant degrees.

Age differences approached, but did not achieve, significance ($p < .10$).
Even so, it was surprising to find that among all groups, the high school

girls were the most positive in portraying both Principal Subjects and Environments while girls in the third grade were the most negative. Elderly men portrayed the most negative Environments.

☐ Gender Differences in the Self-Images, Autonomous Subjects, and Interrelationships Portrayed by Children

This study (Silver, 1992, 2000c) asked three questions: 1) Do boys tend to represent autonomous subjects in their drawings?; 2) Do girls tend to represent subjects interacting with others?; and 3) Do children tend to identify with the subjects of their drawings by choosing principal subjects that are the same gender as themselves?

The SDT responses of 261 children, ages 7–10, in the second through fourth grades were reviewed. Respondents were 145 boys and 116 girls in eight elementary schools in four states and Ontario, Canada, who had responded to the Drawing from Imagination task when normative data was being developed.

This sample of children drew pictures about subjects the same gender as themselves to a degree that was highly significant at the .001 level of probability, supporting the theory that children who respond to projective drawing tasks tend to identify with the principal subjects of their drawings.

In addition, 27% of the girls and 36% of the boys chose animal subjects, which may represent self-images. Since there was no opportunity to talk with the children, their drawings about animals were eliminated from statistical analyses.

No significant gender differences were found in drawings about autonomous principal subjects. Although the proportion of boys (46%) exceeded the proportion of girls (37%), the difference was not significant. Nevertheless, proportionally twice as many boys (28%) as girls (14%) drew self-sufficient subjects actively enjoying themselves. This finding seems to support Gilligan's observation that detachment, and attendant ego-centricism, are associated with the masculine mode.

More girls (29%) than boys (17%) drew pictures about friendly relationships, more boys (19%) than girls (5%) drew assaultive relationships. Virtually no gender differences were found in drawings about caring relationships (girls 16%, boys 14%), although some boys associated caring with living in a dangerous world while all the girls associated caring with living in a pleasant world.

To illustrate caring relationships, consider The Cat who Tried to Save the Rat, Figure 10-1, by Tony with, I Love my Pets, Figure 10-2, by his classmate, Danielle.

FIGURE 10-1. The Cat Who Tried to Save the Rat, by Tony.

FIGURE 10-2. I Love my Pets, by Danielle.

☐ Age and Gender Differences in Attitudes toward Self and Others

Building on the previous findings, this study asked three additional questions: 1) Do response drawings express attitudes toward self and others?; 2) Do males and females have characteristically different attitudes?; and if so, 3) Do their attitudes change from youth, to maturity, to old age? (Silver, 1993b).

Subjects included 531 children, adolescents, and adults in five age groups: 7–10, 13–16, 17–19, 20–50, and 65 and older. The responses were divided into drawings about solitary subjects and drawings about relationships, and then examined for age and gender differences and similarities.

To determine whether the respondents tended to draw pictures about subjects the same gender as themselves, a 2 × 2 chi-square was calculated.

TABLE 10-1. The gender of principal subjects in drawings by 257 men and boys.

Age	No. n	Male Subjects n	%	Female Subjects n	%	Animal Subjects n	%	Unclear n	%
7–10	145	86	59	9	6	50	34	0	
13–16	37	17	46	3	8	17	46	0	
17–19	22	10	45	4	18	8	36	0	
20–50	25	10	40	6	24	5	20	4	16
65+	28	15	54	5	18	7	25	1	4
	N = 257	138	54	27	11	87	34	5	2

TABLE 10-2. The gender of principal subjects in drawings by 274 women and girls.

Age	No. n	Male Subjects n	%	Female Subjects n	%	Animal Subjects n	%	Unclear n	%
7–10	116	12	10	73	63	31	27	0	
13–16	28	5	18	16	57	7	25	0	
17–19	38	5	13	23	61	10	26	0	
20–50	61	6	10	22	39	26	43	5	8
65+	31	3	10	6	19	9	29	13	42
	N = 274	31	11	142	52	83	31	18	7

Those who chose human subjects, drew same-gender subjects to a degree significant at the .001 level of probability ($\chi^2 = 145.839$ $p < .001$; phi coefficient = .657), as shown in Tables 10-1 and 10-2.

Similarity between genders also emerged in using animal subjects to represent people (34% males, 31% females). To illustrate, consider Man Chases Woman as Dog Chases Cat, Figure 10-3, by a man.

Although more females than males portrayed relationships, and more males than females portrayed solitary subjects, these differences did not reach statistical significance, as shown in Table 10-3, but when *attitudes* were taken into account, significant gender differences emerged.

As shown in Tables 10-4 and 10-5, significantly more males than females expressed positive attitudes toward solitary subjects and negative attitudes toward relationships, ($\chi^2 = 46.971$, $p < .001$, phi = .474).

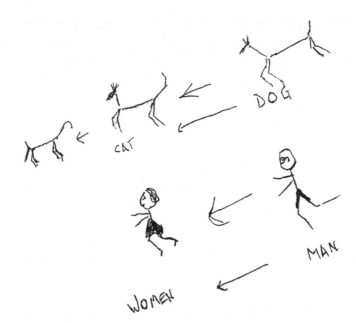

FIGURE 10-3. Man Chases Woman as Dog Chases Cat.

TABLE 10-3. Comparing genders in drawings about solitary subjects and relationships.

| | Drawings by Males | | | | | Drawings by Females | | | | |
| | No. | Solitary S. | | Relationships | | No. | Solitary S. | | Relationships | |
Age	n	n	%	n	%	n	n	%	n	%
7–10	145	67	46	78	54	116	43	37	73	63
13–16	38	15	39	23	61	28	9	32	19	68
17–19	21	6	29	15	71	38	16	42	22	58
20–50	25	12	48	13	52	61	22	36	39	64
65+	28	14	50	14	50	31	16	52	15	48
	N = 257	114	44	143	56	N = 274	106	39	168	61

Total respondents
(Male + Female)
N = 531   114 = 21   143 = 27   106 = 20   168 = 32

Females also expressed positive attitudes toward solitary subjects, but had both positive and negative attitudes toward relationships ($\chi^2 = 25.32$, $p < .001$).

Males of all ages drew assaultive relationships significantly more often than females. However, age and gender differences interacted resulting in

TABLE 10-4. Attitudes toward solitary subjects in responses by boys and men.

Age	No. n	Sad or Helpless		Frustrated or Frightened		Ambivalent, Unemotional or Unclear		Passive Pleasure		Active Pleasure	
		n	%	n	%	n	%	n	%	n	%
7–10	67	3	4	3	4	13	19	29	43	19	28
13–16	15	0		3	20	3	20	3	20	6	40
17–19	6	0		2	33	1	17	2	33	1	17
20–50	12	0		5	42	1	8	2	17	4	33
65+	14	0		3	21	5	36	3	21	3	21
Total	N = 114	3	3	16	14	23	20	39	34	33	29
		Negative: 19	(17%)					Positive: 72	(63%)		

TABLE 10-5. Attitudes toward relationships in responses by boys and men.

Age	No. n	Assaultive		Stressful		Ambivalent, Unemotional or Unclear		Friendly		Caring	
		n	%	n	%	n	%	n	%	n	%
7–10	78	15	19	22	28	17	22	13	17	11	14
13–16	23	8	35	6	26	6	26	2	9	1	4
17–19	15	7	47	5	33	1	7	0		2	13
20–50	13	2	15	4	31	0		1	8	6	46
65+	14	3	21	9	64	1	7	1	7	0	
Total	N = 143	35	25	46	32	25	17	17	12	20	14
		Negative: 81	(57%)					Positive: 37	(26%)		

significant variability in assaultive fantasies for females but not for males ($\chi^2(1) = 9.38$, $p < .01$, and $\chi^2(4) = 13.07$, $p < .05$, respectively).

The converse age and gender interaction was found for caring relationships. Females of all ages drew caring relationships significantly more often than males, whereas males showed significant age variability, as shown in Tables 10-6 and 10-7. The proportion of younger men who drew pictures about caring relationships exceeded the proportion of younger women as well as the proportion of all other male age groups, ($\chi^2(4) = 12.52$, $p < .05$).

When caring and friendly relationships were combined, female age groups excelled (41% female, 26% male). Differences appeared, however, when caring relationships (worth 5 points) and friendly relationships (worth 4 points) were examined separately. The largest proportion of fantasies about caring relationships were drawn by the sample of young men

TABLE 10-6. Attitudes toward solitary subjects in responses by girls and women.

Age	No. n	Sad or Helpless n	%	Frustrated or Frightened n	%	Ambivalent, Unemotional or Unclear n	%	Passive Pleasure n	%	Active Pleasure n	%
7–10	43	2	5	4	9	7	16	24	56	6	14
13–16	9	1	11	0		0		6	67	2	22
17–19	16	0		3	19	2	13	8	50	3	19
20–50	22	1	5	4	18	1	5	10	45	6	27
65+	16	2	13	1	6	6	38	2	13	5	31
Total	N = 106	6	6	12	11	16	15	50	47	22	21
		Negative: 18	(17%)					Positive: 72	(68%)		

TABLE 10-7. Attitudes toward relationships in responses by girls and women.

Age	No. n	Assaultive n	%	Stressful n	%	Ambivalent, Unemotional or Unclear n	%	Friendly n	%	Caring n	%
7–10	73	4	5	29	40	7	10	21	29	12	16
13–16	19	3	16	10	53	2	11	3	16	1	5
17–19	22	5	23	3	14	2	9	6	27	6	27
20–50	39	1	3	16	41	6	15	12	31	4	10
65+	15	4	27	3	20	4	27	2	13	2	13
Total	N = 168	17	10	61	36	21	13	44	26	25	15
		Negative: 78	(46%)					Positive: 69	(41%)		

(46%), a proportion larger than any other male or female age group (see Table 10-5). Approximately twice as many females as males drew friendly relationships (26% female, 12% males; Tables 10-5 and 10-7).

When strongly and moderately negative attitudes toward solitary subjects were combined, no gender differences were found. When separated, however, differences again appeared. A larger proportion of females drew sad or helpless subjects whereas a larger proportion of males drew angry or frightened subjects.

More males than females associated solitary subjects with active pleasures (29% males, 21% females, worth 5 points), more females than males associated solitary subjects with passive pleasures (47% females, 34% males, worth 4 points), the largest proportion appeared among adolescents (Tables 10-4 and 10-6).

Unexpectedly, more senior adults than any other age or gender group drew pictures about stressful relationships or sad, solitary subjects, as shown in Tables 10-5 and 10-6. These findings prompted a closer look at the responses of senior adults, as will be discussed later in this chapter.

Although this study, like the previous study, found a tendency to draw fantasies about same gender subjects, some respondents drew fantasies about subjects of the opposite sex, and surprisingly, portrayed them as menacing or unfortunate. This unexpected finding prompted the next study.

☐ Age and Gender Differences in Attitudes toward the Opposite Sex

This study asked if response drawings about subjects of the opposite sex expressed negative attitudes to a degree that was statistically significant (Silver, 1997, 2000a). If so, the responses might reflect preoccupation with troubling experiences and could provide opportunities for clinical intervention.

With this in mind, the responses of 480 children, adolescents, and adults, were examined. The samples included 222 males and 258 females who had responded to the Stimulus Drawings task or the SDT Drawing from Imagination task. Drawings about the opposite sex were collected, divided into groups based on age and gender, and scored on a rating scale adapted from the SDT Self-Image and Emotional Content scales. The groups were compared, and their mean scores analyzed.

The sample of children, ages 8–11, was students in grades 2 through 5 in five public elementary schools and one private school in New Jersey and New York. The adolescents, ages 12–19, were students in grades 7 through 12 in ten public elementary and high schools in Nebraska, New York, Pennsylvania, and Ohio. This population also included the younger students of a class of college freshmen in Nebraska. The younger adults, ages 20 to 50, were the older college students together with adults in Nebraska, New York, and Wisconsin. The senior adults, ages 65 and above, were living independently in their communities, or attending recreational programs or social occasions in New York and Florida. These respondents totaled 480.

Participants in the study were 116 children and adults, 46 males and 70 females who responded to the tasks by choosing stimulus drawings of the opposite sex, then drawing fantasies about them. An analysis of variance was used to analyze results.

Several age and gender trends emerged. About one in four of the 480 respondents chose stimulus drawings of the opposite sex, the percentages

FIGURE 10-4. Fairy Tales can Come True.

increasing with age from 29% of the children to 44% of the adolescents, to 77% of the adults. The remaining subjects chose animal or same-sex subjects. More men (41%) than women (36%) drew pictures about subjects of the opposite sex whereas the reverse was found among children and adolescents.

Male respondents were significantly more negative than females. In addition, an age difference of borderline significance was found. The children and adolescents were more negative than the adults ($F(1,112) =$ 2.77, $p < .10$). The male mean score was 2.35; the female mean score, 2.94 ($F(1,112) = 6.92$, $p < .01$). There was no interaction.

Both males and females expressed more negative than positive feelings toward the opposite sex. As shown in Figure 10-4 and Table 10-8, males were more negative than females, females more positive than males. Both genders peaked at the 2-point level, drawing moderately negative portrayals of opposite sex subjects that were most often ridiculous or repulsive.

To illustrate, consider the responses shown in Figures 10-5 and 10-6. Fairy Tales can Come True (Fig. 10-4) is the fantasy of a young woman who chose two stimulus drawings, the mouse and the bride. The plump little mouse, crowned and robed, appears to be the bridegroom.

TABLE 10-8. Sex differences in portrayals of the opposite sex.

	46 Males		70 Females	
	n	%	*n*	%
menacing	5	10.9	5	7.1
victim	6	13.0	2	2.9
powerful	6	13.0	5	3.7
ridiculous	12	26.1	19	27.1
unemotional	3	6.5	0	0
ambivalent	3	6.5	7	10.0
unclear	4	8.7	10	14.3
fortunate	3	6.5	8	11.4
friendly	1	2.2	5	7.1
effective	0	0	2	2.9
loving	3	6.5	8	11.4

FIGURE 10-5. Do Not Marry a Refrigerator—it won't be any Fun and it's Probably Not Legal Anyway.

Do Not Marry a Refrigerator... (Fig. 10-5) is the fantasy of a young man who chose the bride and the refrigerator and drew them side by side, presumably at the alter of a church. The bride smiles, the refrigerator door firmly in hand. A top hat on the refrigerator suggests it represents the bridegroom.

FIGURE 10-6. Untitled, by a girl, age 11.

An 11-year old girl responded with the untitled drawing shown in Figure 10-6. Like the young woman, she seems to identify with the bride and to associate the bride with a groom, symbolized by a mouse, but in her drawing, the mouse has become youthful, and offers the bride a bouquet. She seems repelled, judging by her facial expression, rigid arms, and extended fingers.

An 8-year old boy responded with, The Lady Getting Married to a Dog. . ., Figure 10-7. Like the young man, he seemed to associate the groom with passivity (the dog turning away) and the bride with danger (knife in one hand and snakes in her veil).

Although most respondents had negative associations with their subjects of the opposite sex, one seems positive. A 9-year old boy drew, "I came from the refrigerator. . ., Figure 10-8. He chose, and simply copied the girl and refrigerator stimulus drawings, then added the word, "ice" and the person in bed. His use of the pronoun "I" twice in his title, suggests that he may have identified with his female subject.

Although the males in this study expressed significantly more negative feelings toward females than females toward males, they were not necessarily expressing misogyny. If it is typical to project self-images through drawings, then drawings about opposite sex subjects are likely to symbolize the other, not the self.

It was unexpected to find negative feelings so prevalent among both genders. Miller (1997) has suggested that disgust serves to protect selfhood against a variety of intruders, and the challenge of different opinions and value systems. He also points out that disgust marks the boundaries

FIGURE 10-7. The Lady Getting Married to a Dog Who Wants to kill him, by a boy, age 8.

of one's culture and sense of identity. It would seem to follow that feelings of disgust and superiority could be expected in drawings about others, just as drawings about the self tend to elicit positive associations, as found in the previous studies.

It is important to note that only 21% of the males and 27% of the females drew pictures about subjects of the opposite sex. It may be that unhappy experiences with members of the opposite sex were triggered by the stimulus drawings they chose and associated with their fantasies. The findings of this study suggest that opposite sex fantasies in responses to the drawing task could provide access to conflicts or troubling relationships, and thereby, opportunities for clinical discussion and intervention.

☐ Fantasies about Food and Eating

The Sneaky Snacker, an SDT response by a 9-year old girl, and "I tell her not to eat sugar...", by a young mother (Figs. 10-10 and 10-11) made me wonder if response drawings could provide clues to eating disorders.

FIGURE 10-8. I Came from the Refrigerator then I went to Bed, by a boy, age 9.

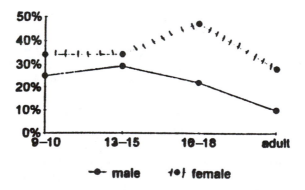

FIGURE 10-9. Age and sex differences in fantasies about food and eating.

Although only two of the 15 SDT stimulus drawings concern food (the soda and the refrigerator), they seemed to be chosen by women and girls more often than other age or gender groups.

To test this hunch, I reviewed the drawings of 293 children, adolescents, and adults who had responded to the SDT in previous studies. The sample

FIGURE 10-10. The Sneaky Snacker, by a girl, age 9.

FIGURE 10-11. I Tell her Not to Eat Sugar/Then I Do, by a young woman.

of children, ages 9–10, included 4th graders in New Jersey, Pennsylvania, and New York. The younger adolescents, ages 12–15, attended grades 7–10 in Nebraska, New York, and Pennsylvania. The older adolescents, ages 16–18, included high school seniors in two public high schools in New York. The adults, ages 19–70, included college students in Nebraska, adults in college audiences in Idaho, New York, and Wisconsin, and older adults living independently in their communities in Florida.

Of the 293 responses, 85 (29%) were fantasies about food or eating. Chi-square analyses indicated that overall, females drew more pictures about food (33.7%) than males (22%) in each of the four age groups, as shown in Figure 10-9. This difference reached borderline significance (Chi-square (1) = 3.31, $p < .10$).

One other difference was found. When scores of the older adolescents and adults were combined, the gender difference (14.6% for males, 33.33% for females) also reached borderline significance (Chi-square (1) = 4.25, $p < .05$.).

Among females, the largest proportion of drawings about food or eating emerged in the sample of older adolescents (46.9%), followed by the samples of younger girls (34.4%), and women (27.9%).

Among males, the largest proportion emerged in the sample of younger adolescents ages 13–15, (29.4%), followed by boys ages 9–10 (25%); by older adolescents ages 16–18, (22.2%); and finally, by men (10%).

The most notable gender difference appeared in neutral responses (ambivalent, ambiguous, or unclear): 45% of the females, compared with 23% of the males, received this intermediate numerical score.

The findings of this study suggest that the SDT Drawing from Imagation task might be useful in screening for masked bulimia or anorexia nervosa, and that further study would be worthwhile.

☐ Gender Differences in the Spatial Abilities of Adolescents

It is often assumed that females lag behind males in spatial ability. It has even been claimed that male superiority is not just confirmed but not even in dispute (Moir and Jessel, 1992). According to McGee (1979), years of psychological testing have yielded a consensus on male superiority, including concepts of horizontality and verticality.

Unwilling to accept these assumptions, two studies compared male and female responses to the SDT Drawing from Observation and Predictive Drawing tasks.

The first study compared the SDT responses of 33 girls and 33 boys, ages 12–15, attending public schools in Nebraska, Pennsylvania, and New York

TABLE 10-9. Significant differences between male and female adolescents in spatial ability using the Silver Drawing Test (Silver, 1996c).

Dependent Measure	Subjects Females n	Males n	Mean Females n	Males n	Std. Dev. Females n	Males n	Degrees of Freedom	Value of t	Significance
Sequence	33	33	4.48	4.55	0.83	0.87	64	−0.29	n.s.
Horizontal	33	32	4.12	4.22	0.99	0.97	63	−0.40	n.s.
Vertical	33	33	2.85	2.42	1.64	1.56	64	1.08	n.s.
LR	33	33	4.24	4.18	0.79	1.01	64	0.27	n.s.
AB	33	33	4.18	4.06	0.68	0.75	64	0.69	n.s.
FB	33	33	3.70	3.06	1.10	1.56	64	1.91	$p < 1.0$
Total	33	32	23.58	22.31	3.47	3.57	63	1.45	n.s.

(Silver, 1996c). Their mean scores were analyzed using a computation of t-test scores.

No significant differences in spatial ability emerged (see Table 10-9). The statistical test (MANOVA) indicated no overall gender differences on spatial measures. The girls received higher mean scores on horizontality, verticality, depth, and above-below relationships. Boys had higher mean scores in sequencing and left-right relationships.

If it is true that males consistently excel in spatial ability, how can these responses to the SDT be explained? A possible explanation may lie in the experiment by Thomas, Jamison, & Hammer (1973) who reported that college women, previously unaware that the surface of still water in a bottle remains horizontal, failed to learn the concept. The women were shown an apparatus consisting of a bottle half-filled with water and a "pretend bottle," then asked to adjust the pretend waterline to the position that the real water had taken.

Piaget and Inhelder noted that horizontality is learned by noticing parallels. They presented their students with jars of tinted water on a table at eye level, then asked their students to guess the position water would take when the bottle was tilted. Next, they asked students to draw what they observed. They took care to make their students include the edge of the table in their drawing, and presented the water level at eye level, or slightly above, to help them observe (Piaget & Inherder, 1967, p. 381).

In reading the report by Thomas et al. (1973) I noticed that their illustration showed someone adjusting the position of bottles attached to vertical disks mounted on vertical boards. There is no table and the bottles are below eye level. Apparently, a critical clue for discovering horizontality was missing—an external horizontal frame of reference.

The SDT Predictive Drawing task provides an external horizontal frame of reference with the line representing the table surface, as discussed by Piaget and Inhelder. The experiment by Thomas et al apparently failed to do so, thus discouraging, rather than encouraging, the women's discovery of horizontality (Silver, 1978).

☐ Gender Parity and Disparity in Performing Spatial Tasks

The second study pursued the question of why some studies found females failing to perform in spatial tasks. These studies had judged performances on the basis of success or failure—either she knew or did not know that the surface of still water is horizontal, or that a plumbline, or house on a hill remains vertical.

The present study asked whether different approaches to scoring affected the findings (Silver, 1998b). Subjects were 176 participants (88 male and 88 females). The adult sample was made up of 26 men and 26 women, ages 18–50 years (mean age 26), who had responded to the SDT tasks in previous studies. The adolescent subjects were the 33 girls and 33 boys who had participated in the previous study. The group of children who participated was made up of 29 girls and 29 boys, all 4th graders, ages 9–11 in New Jersey, Pennsylvania, and New York schools.

The respondents drawings were rescored in terms of success or failure, the approach used in the reports of female failure. Only those who drew horizontal lines in the tilted bottle or vertical houses on the hill, were deemed successful. Chi-square analyses were conducted on the proportions of males and females who succeeded, as well as those who failed.

Again, no significant gender differences were found in either success-failure scores or cognitive level scores. Although proportionally more males than females succeeded, the difference did not reach statistical significance. As shown in Tables 10-10 to 10-12, the chi-square analysis indicated that the probability was less than .10 (borderline). Both males and females had lower scores in verticality than in horizontality.

High scores increased with age among both genders, as low scores decreased. None of the adults failed the horizontality task but seven (27%) of the men and four (15%) of the women failed the verticality task. Of the seven men who received the lowest score of 1 point in verticality, four scored 5 points in horizontality. Of the four women who scored 1 in verticality, two scored 5 in horizontality.

TABLE 10-10. Success-failure assessment of responses to the SDT horizontality task.

		Males					Females			
		3 Points		1 Point			3 Points		1 Point	
	No.					No.				
Age Group	n	n	%	n	%	n	n	%	n	%
18–50	26	19	73	0		26	13	38	11	
12–13	33	14	39	2	6	33	12	36	2	6
9–11	27	6	22	3	19	23	3	19	9	35
Total	86	39	43	7	8	84	32	38	11	13

Note: Success = horizontal line in the tilted bottle (3 points); Failure = line parallels bottom or side of the tilted bottle (1 point).

TABLE 10-11. Success-failure assessment of responses to the SDT verticality task.

Age Group	No. n	Males 5 Points n	5 Points %	1 Point n	1 Point %	No. n	Females 5 Points n	5 Points %	1 Point n	1 Point %
18–50	26	11	42	7	27	26	7	27	4	13
12–15	33	6	18	14	42	33	8	24	11	33
9–11	27	1	4	16	39	23	0		8	31
Total	86	18	21	37	43	84	13	18	23	27

Note: Success = vertical house on the spot marked X (5 points); Failure = perpendicular house on the spot marked X (1 point).

TABLE 10-12. Gender differences in responses to the SDT horizontal and vertical tasks.

SDT Score	Gender Males	Females
Verticality		
1 (fail)	43.1%*	27.4%*
3 (pass)	20.9%	17.9%
Horizontality		
1 (fail)	8.1%	10.1%
3 (pass)	45.3%	38.1%

*Chi-square (df =1) = 2.93, $p < .10$.

In analyzing the developmental levels of test performances, new data from the children were combined with previous data from the adolescents and adults. t-tests were conducted on the mean scores to determine whether there were gender differences when the entire sample was considered as a whole.

Again, no significant gender differences were found (means for horizontality: males 4.08, females, 3.88; for verticality, males 2.57, females 2.83). When the sample for analysis consisted of children and adolescents under the age of 16, there was a borderline significant gender effect ($t(115) =$

1.68, $p < .10$) for verticality; female children and adolescents had a mean of 2.55, males 3.12. In the sample of adults, no gender differences were found.

To summarize, this study found no significant gender differences in performing the horizontality and verticality tasks. Changing the form of assessment did not change the results.

How can discrepancies between findings be explained? One possible explanation may be low expectations. Lower expectations of achievement lead to lower achievement. The typical female pattern of attributing success to luck, rather than capability, fosters low expectancies for achievment, and consequently, poor performance.

A second possible explanation may be that investigators who found female failure were testing knowledge of physical phenomena. Piaget and Inhelder who originated the tasks, emphasized differences between knowledge of physics and knowledge of "natural reference systems such as the horizontals and verticals, which were tested in their tasks and the SDT tasks which also replicated them."

The 1998 study also examined individual responses to the drawing task. An art director and a gifted 9-year old received the highest scores whereas some adults with graduate degrees received low scores.

Training is usually expected to improve task performance. Training in spatial skills is usually provided by art teachers in elementary and secondary schools. Concepts of horizontality and verticality are fundamental in art experience, as evident in the stereotype of an artist sighting along a brush held vertically at arms length. Many schools however, do not provide education in art, and art is usually the first subject to go when school budgets are cut. These schools may fail to meet the needs of students who may be deficient in spatial skills and students who may be gifted in this area.

The findings of this study call into question the widespread assumption of male superiority in spatial intelligence. They suggest that nonverbal expression through drawng offers unique opportunities to contribute to the growing body of knowledge about age and gender differences and similarities.

☐ Comparing Attitudes and Spatial Abilities of Aging and Young Adults

As reported earlier, more elderly men drew fantasies about stressful relationships than any other age or gender group, and more elderly women drew more fantasies about sad solitary subjects (Silver, 1993b). This study took a closer look at these findings by reexamining the responses of 59 seniors.

The subjects were 28 men and 31 women, age 65 or older, living independently in their communities. One group (18 men and 18 women) had responded to the Stimulus Drawings task while attending a recreational program for seniors in New York. The other group (9 men and 13 women) had responded to the SDT Drawing from Imagination task while attending a similar program in Florida.

The findings indicated that the proportion of senior men who drew fantasies about stressful relationships (64%) was twice the proportion of all male age groups combined (32%), as shown in Table 10-5. In addition, more than three times as many senior men as senior women (20%) drew stressful relationships (Table 10-7). Total population scores eclipsed these age and gender differences.

To put this finding in perspective, humor appeared more often in responses by seniors than that of any other age group and more often in responses by senior men (39%) than senior women (16%). Furthermore, the humor tended to be self-deprecating, as discussed in Chapter 3.

In addition, two surprising reversals emerged. Proportionally, more senior men (54%) than senior women (19%) drew fantasies about subjects the same gender as themselves, reversing the trend found in other age groups. Same gender subjects had peaked among the youngest boys (59%), and then gradually declined to approximately 40% of the young men and women. This may suggest that preoccupation with self declines with maturity, but while the decline continued among older women, it reversed among older men (Tables 10-1 and 10-2).

More males than females drew fantasies about solitary subjects engaged in active pleasures, and more females than males drew fantasies about solitary subjects engaged in passive pleasures. When age groups were examined, however, the senior women reversed the trend. The findings showed that 31% drew solitary subjects engaged in active pleasures. The senior women drew more fantasies about daring escapades than all other groups combined, as shown in Tables 10-4 and 10-6.

In the literature, only one reference to similar observations has been found, a newspaper report of a Grandmother's Festival in Norway attended by hundreds of older women who wanted to test their limits with activities such as jumping from horses and leaping from airplanes. As one of the participants explained, older women are at a stage in their lives when they have fewer responsibilities and, therefore, can take such risks.

I am acquainted with a woman in a retirement community who asked if she might ride in a hot air balloon, as a special gift for her 90th birthday. Her wish was granted, and the experience gave her so much pleasure that she requested another balloon ride for her 91st birthday. These findings led to the study that follows.

☐ Differences among Aging and Young Men and Women in Attitudes and Cognition

This study was undertaken because of the need to challenge stereotypes and misconceptions about aging (Silver, 1999b). Much is known about senior adults in nursing homes, but little is known about those who remain physically, financially, and psychologically independent. Researchers tend to study nursing home residents, perhaps because these residents are readily available, or may feel unable to decline. This could explain why research on aging has tended to emphasize losses.

To compare independent seniors with young adults in cognitive skills as well as attitudes, groups of seniors were asked if they would participate in a study of age and gender differences by responding anonymously to pencil-and-paper drawing tasks that did not require art skills. Those who volunteered became the self-selected sample ($N = 57$) of senior adults for this study. Their ages ranged from 64–95 years with a mean age of 80.8 years. All lived independently in their own homes or in two retirement residences.

Twenty seniors lived in **Community A** which provided many amenities; 16 of the 20 had college degrees. Twenty lived in **Community B**, which provided fewer amenities and charged minimal fees. Although they were not asked about educational backgrounds, a staff member believed that few had attended college. Ten additional seniors lived independently in their own homes in upper middle class socioeconomic neighborhoods, all having attended college. Fourteen seniors responded to the drawing tasks during an art class provided by a recreational program. Their educational and economic backgrounds were unknown. All seemed in reasonably good health and all lived in Florida.

Subjects for the study included 57 senior and 51 younger adults (a class of college freshmen from Nebraska and volunteers in two college audiences in New York and Idaho) who responded to two SDT tasks, Drawing from Imagination and Predictive Drawing. The sample of younger adults was made up of 18 men and 33 women who had responded to the drawing tasks in previous studies. Their ages ranged between 20–50 years with a mean age of 28.7. They included a class of college freshmen in Nebraska, and volunteers in two college audiences, one in New York, the other in Idaho. Responses to the drawing from imagination task were scored for Cognitive and Emotional Content.

No significant age differences were found between the independent seniors and younger adults in responding to the Drawing from Imagination
task. Gender differences, however, emerged.[1]

---

[1]The first analysis examined the scores of 95 subjects who responded to the SDT Drawing
from Imagination task. These subjects were 17 male and 27 female senior adults, and 18
male and 33 female young adults.

A second analysis examined the scores of 73 individuals who responded to the SDT
Predictive Drawing task: 10 male and 26 female seniors, 6 male and 32 female young
adults.

A third analysis examined Predictive Drawing scores of 206 subjects in four age groups:
53 children, 66 adolescents, 51 young adults, and 36 seniors.

Gender and age group were the variables of interest in an Analysis of Variance. They
included Emotional Content, Self-Image, and Cognitive Content in responses to the Drawing
from Imagination task, and Horizontality, Verticality, and Sequencing in responses to the
Predictive Drawing task.

The first study included 95 individuals (17 men and 27 women in the senior age group, 18
men and 33 women in the young adult group). There were no significant effects for age group
in responses to the Drawing from Imagination task. For gender, however, a significant effect
emerged in Self-Image scores ($F(1,91) = 4.61$, $p < .05$). Males had significantly higher scores
(stronger self-images) than females (3.66 and 3.20, respectively). In Emotional Content
scores, a borderline significant effect of gender emerged ($F(1,91) = 3.20$, $p < .10$). Females
had significantly higher scores (portraying fortunate individuals or caring relationships more
often than males (3.24 and 2.77, respectively).

In a study of the Predictive Drawing scores of 73 individuals (10 men and 26 women in
the senior age group, 6 men and 32 women in the young adult group) there was a trend
toward an age group difference in horizontality ($F(1,69) = 2.75$, $p < .15$.). Young adults
had a higher score than senior adults (4.95 and 4.37, respectively). Gender differences in
horizontality also emerged ($F(1,69) = 8.14$, $p < .01$). Males scored higher than females (4.95
and 4.37, respectively).

Similarly, in ability to sequence, significant gender differences were found ($F(1,69) = 4.23$,
$p < .05$). Males scored significantly higher than females (4.70 and 3.74, respectively).

To further analyze for potential age difference, the sample was expanded to include four
age groups (53 children, 66 adolescents, 36 seniors, 51 young adults). Several age trends
emerged.

For horizontality, there was a significant effect of age group ($F(1,196) = 18.61$, $p < .0001$).
Children (3.15) scored less than adolescents (4.17). Adolescents scored less than young adults
(4.61) but did not differ from seniors (4.49). The young adults and senior adults did not differ.

For verticality, a main effect for age group emerged ($F(1,197) = 12.30$, $p < .001$). Children
(1.98) scored less than adolescents (2.64) who in turn scored less than adults (3.53) and
seniors (3.32). The adult groups did not differ.

For ability to sequence, there was a borderline significant effect ($F(1,147) = 2.68$, $p < .10$).
Adolescents scored significantly higher than seniors (4.52 vs. 3.95). Young adults scored in
the middle (4.15) and did not differ from either group. Gender differences were also observed
but not detailed here.

In general, it appears that there are few age-related changes in SDT performances. There
may be a slight trend towards a decline in horizontality scores, but more study is needed to
test this hypothesis.

Drawing from Imagination

The seniors had higher cognitive scores than the young adults, but the difference did not reach significance. In top ranges scores, 57% of the seniors, compared with 41% of the young adults, received the highest scores, as shown Figure 10-12 in Chart 1.

Predictive Drawing

In verticality, no significant age differences were found, but proportionally more younger adults received top scores (54% and 15%, respectively), a finding that was not apparent in the statistical analysis. On the other hand, more seniors received the next highest score (35% vs. 19%), drawing vertical houses on the mountain slope without providing adequate support.

These drawings could be metaphors for feeling unsteady on one's feet, so often experienced in old age. Perhaps drawing an unstable house on a slope reflects an age-related change in the perception of verticality. Education, also, may have influenced the verticality scores. The seniors were compared with young adults many of whom were attending college (the educational background of many of the seniors was unknown). The study of Brazilian children and adults by Allessandrini et al (1998) cited earlier, found that college-educated adults had higher SDT scores than those with high school educations.

In horizontality, age differences approached but did not reach significance. More young than old adults scored in the top 5-point range (71% vs. 57%).

In sequencing and horizontality, men had significantly higher scores than women. Perhaps Predictive Drawing triggers thoughts about the objective world whereas Drawing from Imagination triggers thoughts and feelings about the subjective world, eliciting gender differences rather than age differences.

Emotional Content and Self-Images

The scores of both age groups followed similar patterns, as shown in Figure 10-12, Charts 3 and 4. Self-image scores peaked sharply at the 3-point level (ambiguous, ambivalent, or unemotional)

seniors received higher scores than younger adults (Fig. 10-12, Chart 4). This finding suggests that the seniors tended to be more detached and less emotionally involved that the young adults.

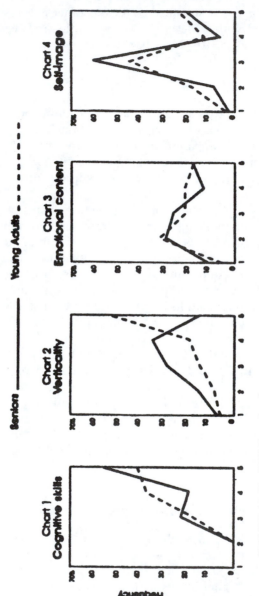

FIGURE 10-12. SDT Drawing from Imagination and verticality scores of senior and young adults.

174

FIGURE 10-13. There I was, all dressed for the costume party, a princess, no less. My little sister couldn't stop giggling. She had helped me raid the attic. I was really puzzled until I felt a movement in my crown. There was a little mouse caught in the wires. We carefully removed him and put him back in the attic—the little prince mouse, by a woman, age 80.

As measured by the Self-Image scale, men had significantly higher scores, drawing more fantasies about powerful or effective principal subjects, suggesting stronger self-images, as found in previous studies.

As measured by the Emotional Content scale, women had higher scores, drawing more fantasies about fortunate individuals and caring relationships, as found in previous studies. The drawing shown in Figure 10-13 is the response of a woman age 80, who chose the mouse and princess from the SDT array. She wrote:

> There I was all dressed for the costume party, a princess no less. My little sister couldn't stop giggling. She had helped me raid the attic. I was really puzzled until I felt a movement in my crown. There was a little mouse caught in the wires. We carefully removed him and put him back in the attic—the little prince mouse.

This response received the highest score in Emotional Content because it represents caring relationships. It also received the highest score on the self-image scale because her use of the pronoun "I" indicates that she identified with her fortunate principal subject. In adddition, she received the top score in cognitive skills (ability to select, combine, and represent), having represented an imaginative, and well-organized fantasy or recollection.

FIGURE 10-14. The Snake and the Mouse, by a man, age 82.

The Snake and the Mouse (Fig. 10-14) was the humorous response of a man, age 82. Since his meaning is ambiguous and his protagonist, unclear, he received the intermediate, neutral score in both Emotional Content and Self-Image. With no opportunity to discuss his meanings, either the snake, the mouse, or the narrator could be self-images. The snake's embrace could be disastrous for the mouse or delicious for the snake. At any event, his drawing transforms the stimulus drawings of a snake and the mouse and is original, playful, and suggestive, receiving top scores in the cognitive skills assessed by the drawing task.

Senior Women in Communities A and B

The unanticipated finding of differences between genders, not age, prompted a closer look at the performances of the senior women. The 13 women in Community A had higher mean scores in both horizontality and sequencing than the 13 women in Community B (4.38 vs. 3.74 and 3.69 vs. 3.38, respectively). Although the two groups were similar in age, averaging 79 and 80 years, and initially, both were physically and financially independent, the residents of Community A were more likely to remain independent. They also received additional services—weekly housekeeping, community dining room, staff on call 24-hours a day, assisted living, and a nursing home on the campus.

In Community B, the staff departed at 4 o'clock in the afternoon. If a resident became ill, a court-appointed guardian could force her to leave. To avoid nursing homes, some residents tried to hide their health problems, or refused medical care. Perhaps dread of becoming incapacitated, and anxiety about the future, played a role in the cognitive functioning of residents in Community B. Educational inequality also may also have affected their scores.

To summarize, no significant age differences were found between the samples of independent seniors and young adults. The findings seem to challenge false beliefs about the losses of aging, and support the view that cognitive skills and emotions tend to remain stable into old age unless extrinsic factors intervene, such as losing one's independence. The findings also suggest that the fear of losing autonomy has adverse effects, and being able to maintain independence may be crucial to successful aging.

Further investigation with larger samples of independent seniors may clarify whether those who participated in this study were special populations, or whether their performances were typical of aging adults who are able to sustain their autonomy and independence.

☐ Cultural Differences and Similarities

Brazil and the United States

The SDT was standardized on approximately 2,000 Brazilian children and adults by Allessandrini, Duarte, Dupas, and Bianco (1998) who also compared their findings with those reported in the SDT test manual (Silver, 1996a). The Brazilian findings confirmed the dependence of cognitive scores on level of education, and their independence from gender. An analyses of variance yielded differences in school grade and type of school at the .001 level of probability. Adults whose education had been limited to elementary or high school had lower mean scores than most children. College graduates had higher mean scores than high school seniors, and private school students had significantly higher scores than public school students. These Brazilian investigators also found high correlations among the SDT subtests and total scores.

The trend of growth in mean scores was similar in both (Brazilian and USA) cultures, increasing gradually with age and grade level. The Brazilian children, ages 5–17, included subgroups based on grade, gender, and type of school. The adults, ages 18–40 were grouped on the basis of educational background. Each subgroup included at least 35 subjects. An analysis of variance yielded differences in school grade and type of school both at the .001 level of significance.

In emotional content, the authors found more negative than positive responses and a high rate of ambivalence among adults. They suggested this latter result could demonstrate a tendency to see both sides of an issue. They also found a tendency toward strongly and moderately negative themes by students in the seventh and eighth grades, with the least tendency of negative themes among 12 graders.

Unfortunately, the Brazilian investigators do not seem to have examined gender differences. Our findings of male mean scores in Emotional

Content parallel the Brazilian tendency toward negative themes, whereas our female mean scores tend to parallel their finding of a high rate of ambivalence, that is, our female scores tend to fall in the intermediate range, defined in the SDT as ambivalent, ambiguous, or unemotional (Silver, 2000c).

The Brazilian investigators performed studies of interscorer and test-retest reliability. Three judges, working independently, scored responses by 32 children in all school grades. The correlation coefficients were .94, .95, and .95 in total SDT scores, indicating very strong interscorer reliability. In retest reliability, the test was administered twice to a group of 44 subjects after an interval of 15–30 days. The results showed test-retest reliability with correlation coefficients ranging from .62 to .87.

Australia

Hunter (1992) administered the SDT to 193 college students (128 women and 65 men, ages 15–53) in Australia. The men predominated in engineering and construction courses; the women, in office and education courses.

Hunter (1992) distinguished between two kinds of spatial thinking—restricted thinking, defined as solving problems that have correct solutions, as in the Predictive Drawing and Drawing from Observation subtests, and unrestricted thinking, defined as creative solutions that are more satisfying to the examinee, as in the Drawing from Imagination subtest. She examined 11 variables within the subtests, using the mean ratings of two scorers as subject data, and a multivariate analysis of variance design.

Gender differences emerged in both restricted and unrestricted spatial thinking. The performances of women appeared superior to the performances of men in Drawing from Imagination and Drawing from Observation.[2]

Hunter observed that these findings were consistent with the theory that cognitive skills evident in verbal conventions can be evident also in visual conventions, and that gender differences should be considered in developing course methodologies in order to facilitate learning.

---

[2]The contrast of gender using the multivariate set of DVs was highly significant ($F(1,150) = 5.8$, $p < .001$). The associated univariate F test for Drawing from Imagination also was significant ($F(1,150) = 13.3$, $p < .001$, Eta 2 = .08). In addition, the associated univariate F test for Drawing from Observation was significant ($F(1,150) = 7.7$, $p < .006$, Eta = .05).

Russia

An art therapist in Russia, Alexander Kopytin, has translated the SDT for use in a cross-cultural study. At this writing, three Russian psychologists are administering the SDT to collect normative data and correlate it with norms based on Russian assessments. After estimating mean scores of students at different age and grade levels, they plan to administer the SDT to students with learning disabilities, dyslexia, and hearing impairments, as well as psychiatric patients and artistically gifted children.

☐ Concluding Observations

This book began with the premise that emotions and cognitive skills can be expressed, assessed, and developed through drawings. The studies presented seem to support the premise. It is hoped that the studies and procedures used will contribute to our understanding of why and how art experience can enhance both therapy and education.

References

Allen, P. B. (1995). *Art is a way of knowing*. Boston: Shambola Publications.

Allessandrini, C. D., Duarte, J. L., Dupas, M. A., & Bianco, M. F. (1998). SDT: The Brazilian standardization of the Silver Drawing Test of Cognition and Emotion. *ARTherapy, Journal of the American Art Therapy Asociation*, 15(2), 107–115.

American Psychiatric Association. (1994). *Diagnostic and statistical manual of mental disorders* (4th ed.). Washington, DC: Author.

Arnheim, R. (1969). *Visual thinking*. CA: University of California Press.

Bannatyne, A. (1971). *Language, reading, and learning disabilities*. Springfield, IL: Charles C. Thomas.

Beck, A. T. (1978). *Depression inventory*. Philadelphia: Philadelphia Center for Cognitive Therapy.

Blasdel, L. (1997). *Critical thinking skills developed through visual art experiences*. Unpublished master's thesis, Emporia State University, Kansas.

Brandt, M. (1995). *Visual stories: A comparison study utilizing the Silver art therapy assessment with adolescent sex offenders*. Unpublished master's thesis, Ursuline College, Pepper Pike, Ohio.

Brenner, C. A. (1974). *Elementary textbook of psychoanalysis*. New York: Anchor Books.

Bruner, J. S. (Ed.), (1966). *Studies in cognitive growth*. New York: John Wiley & Sons.

Coffey, C. M. (1995). *Women, major depression, and imagery*. Unpublished master's thesis, Southern Illinois University, Edwardsville, Illinois.

Damasio, A. R. (1994). *Descartes error*. New York: G. P. Putman's Sons.

Dissanayake, E. (1992). Homoaestheticus: where air comes from and why. *N.Y. Free Press*.

Dunn-Snow, P. (1994). Adapting the Silver Draw A Story assessment: Art therapy techniques with children and adolescents. *American Journal of Art Therapy, 33*, 35–36.

Dubos, R. NY Times, Oct. 17, 1971, p. 56.

Gantt, L. (1990). *A validity study of the Formal Elements Art Therapy Scale (FEATS)*. Unpublished doctoral dissertation, University of Pittsburg, Pennsylvania.

Gardner, H. (1993). *Multiple intelligences*. New York: Basic Books.

Gilligan, C., Ward, D., & Taylor, J. M. (1988). *Mapping the moral domain*. Cambridge, MA: Harvard University Press.

Hayes, K. (1978). *The relationship between drawing ability and reading scores*. Unpublished master's Thesis, College of New Rochelle, New York.

Henn, K. (1990). *The effects of an integrated arts curriculum on the representation of spatial relationships*. Unpublished master's thesis, Buffalo State College, New York.

Hiscox, A. R. (1990). *An alternative to language-oriented IQ tests for learning-disabled children*. Unpublished master's thesis, College of Notre Dame, Belmont, California.

Hoffman, D. D. (1998). *Visual intelligence: How we create what we see*. New York: Norton.

Horovitz-Darby, E. (1996). Preconference course presentation. 1996 Conference of the American Art Therapy Association.

Hunter, G. (1992). *An examination of some individual differences in information processing, personality, and motivation with respect to some dimensions of spatial thinking or problem solving in TAFE students*. Unpublished master's thesis, The University of New England, School of Professional Studies, Armidale, New South Wales, Australia.

Jakobson, R. (1964). Linguistic typology of aphasic impairment. In A. DeReuck & M. O'Conner (Eds.), *Disorder of language*. Boston: Little, Brown & Co.

Jung, C. G. (1974). *Man and his symbols*. New York: Dell Publishing.

Kaplan, F. F. (2000). *Art, science, and art therapy*. London. Jessica Kingsley.

Kramer, E. (1993). *Art as therapy with children*. New York: Schocken Books.

Lachman-Chapin, M. (1987). A self psychology approach to art therapy, In *Approaches to Art Therapy*, G. Rubin (ed.).

Langer, S. K. (1957). *Problems of art*. NY: Charles Scribner & Sons.

Langer, S. K. (1958). *Philosophy in a new key*. New York: Mentor Books.

Langer, S. K. (1962). *Reflections on art*. Baltimore: John Hopkins Press.

Ledoux, J. (1996). *The emotional brain*. New York: Touchstone.

Levick, M. F. (1989). The Levick Emotional and Cognitive Art Therapy Assessment (LECATA). Unpublished document, Supported by the Dade County Div. of Exceptional Student Ed. Clinical.

Linebaugh, A. J. (1996). *What the school age child perceives in a hospital environment: The DAS instrument with physically ill children*. Unpublished master's thesis, Long Island University, C. W. Post Campus, Brookville, New York.

Malchiodi, C. A. (1997). *Breaking the silence*. New York: Brunner/Mazel.

Malchiodi, C. A. (1998). *Understanding children's drawings*. New York: Guilford Press.

Marshall, S. B. (1988). *The use of art therapy to foster cognitve skills with learning disabled children*. Unpublished master's thesis, Pratt Institute, School of Arts and Design, Brooklyn, New York.

McGee, M. (1979). Human spatial abilities: Psychometric studies and environmental influences. *Psychological Bulletin, 86*(5), 889–918.

McKnew, H., Cytryn, L., & Yahries, H. (1983). *Why isn't Johnny crying?* New York: W. W. Norton.

Miller, W. I. (1997). *The anatomy of disgust*. Cambridge, MA: Harvard University Press.

Moir, A. & Jessel, D. (1992). *Brain sex*. New York: Dell.

Moser, J. (1980). *Drawing and painting and learning disabilities*. Unpublished doctoral dissertation, New York University, New York.

Pannunzio, D. M. (1991). *Short-term adjunctive art therapy as a treatment intervention for depressed hospitalized youth*. Unpublished master's thesis, Ursuline College #1031, Pepper Pike, Ohio.

Pfeffer, C. R. (1986). *The suicidal child*. New York: The Guilford Press.

Piaget, J. (1970). *Genetic epistemology*. New York: Columbia University Press.

Piaget, J. & Inhelder, B. (1967). *The child's conception of space*. New York: W. W. Norton.

Restak, R. M. (1994). *The modular brain*. New York: Charles Scribner's Sons.

Rubin, J. A. (1987). *Approaches to Art Therapy*. Brunner/Mazel: New York.

Rubin, J. A. (1999). *Art therapy: An introduction*. Philadelphia: Brunner/Mazel.

Sandburg, L., Silver, R., & Vilstrup, K. (1984). The stimulus drawing technique with adult psychiatric patients, stroke patients, and adolescents in art therapy. *Art Therapy: Journal of the American Art Therapy Association,* 1(3), 132–140.

Schlain, L. (1998). *The alphabet versus the goddess*. New York: Penguin Books.

Shafer, D. & Fisher, P. (1981). The epidemiology of suicide in children and young adolescents. *Journal of the American Academy of Child Psychiatry, 21,* 545–565.

Silver, R. (1967). *A demonstration project in art education for deaf and hard of hearing children and adults*. U.S. Office of Education, Bureau of Research, Project #6-8598. ERIC ED# oi3 009.

Silver, R. (1973). *A study of cognitive skills development through art experiences*. New York: New York City Board of Education. N. Y. State Urban Education Project # 147 232 101. ERIC Ed # 084 745, EC 060 575.

Silver, R. (1975a). *Using art to evaluate and develop cognitive skills*. Paper presented at the 1975 AATA Annual Conference, Louisville, KY. ERIC ED # 116 401. EC 080 793.

Silver, R. (1975b). Children with communication disorders: Cognitive and artistic development. *American Journal of Art Therapy,* 14(2), 39–47.

Silver, R. (1975c). Clues to cognitive functioning in the drawings of stroke patients. *American Journal of Art Therapy, 15*(10), 3–8.

Silver, R. (1976a). *Shout in silence, visual arts and the deaf.* New York: The Metropolitan Museum of Art.

Silver, R. (1976b). Using art to evaluate and develop cognitive skills: Children with communication disorders and children with learning disabilities. *American Journal of Art Therapy, 16*(1), 11–19.

Silver, R. (1978). *Developing cognitive and creative skills through art: Programs for children with communication disorders.* Baltimore: University Park Press. Author' Guild Backinprint.com Edition. iuniverse.com. ERIC ED # 410 479 209 878.

Silver, R. (1979). *Art as language for the handicapped,* Catalogue of an exhibition circulated 1979–1982. Washington, DC: The Smithsonian Institution. ERIC ED # 185 774.

Silver, R. (1981). Stimulus Drawings & Techniques, Ablin Press, Mmaroneck, NY. Revised editions published in 1986, 1989, 1991, 1997 by Ablin Press Distributors.

Silver, R. (1981a). *Stimulus drawings and techniques in therapy, development, and assessment.* New York: Trillium Books, Florida: Ablin Press Distributors.

Silver, R. (1982a). *Stimulus drawings and techniques in therapy, development, and assessment.* New York: Trillium Books, Florida: Ablin Press Distributors.

Silver, R. (1982b). Developing cognitive skills through art. In L. G. Katz (Ed.), *Current topics in early childhood education,* Vol 4 (pp. 143–171). NJ: Ablex Publishing. ERIC ED # 207674.

Silver, R. A. (1983a). Identifying gifted handicapped children through their drawings. *ART Therapy, Journal of the American Art Therapy Association, 1*(10), 40–46. ERIC EJ #295 217.

Silver, R. (1983b). Silver Drawing Test of cognition and Emotion, Seattle, WA: Special Child Publications (first edition).

Silver, R. (1986). *Developing Cognitive Creative Skills in Art,* 2nd Ed. New York: Trillium Press.

Silver, R. (1986a). *Developing cognitive and creative skills through art: Programs for children with communication disorders.* Baltimore: University Park Press. Author' Guild Backinprint.com Edition. iuniverse.com. ERIC ED # 410 479 209 878.

Silver, R. (1986b). *Stimulus drawings and techniques in therapy, development, and assessment.* New York: Trillium Books, Florida: Ablin Press Distributors.

Silver, R. (1987). Draw A Story, Screening for Depression (first edition. Revised editions published in 1988, and 1993, by Ablin Press Distributors, Sarasota, FL.

Silver, R. (1987a). Sex differences in the emotional content of drawings. *Art Therapy: Journal of the American Art Therapy Association, 4*(2), 67–77.

Silver, R. (1987b). *Draw a Story: Screening for depression and age or gender differences.* New York: Trillium Press; Florida, Ablin Press Distributors.

Silver, R. (1988a). Screening children and adolescents for depression through Draw a Story. *American Journal of Art Therapy, 26*(4), 119–124.

Silver, R. (1988b). *Draw a Story: Screening for depression and age or gender differences.* New York: Trillium Press; Florida, Ablin Press Distributors.

Silver, R. (1989). *Developing cognitive and creative skills through art: Programs for children with communication disorders.* Baltimore: University Park Press. Author' Guild Backinprint.com Edition. iuniverse.com. ERIC ED # 410 479 209 878.

Silver, R. (1989). *Stimulus drawings and techniques in therapy, development, and assessment.* New York: Trillium Books, Florida: Ablin Press Distributors.

Silver, R. (1990). *Silver Drawing Test of cognition and emotion.* Seattle, WA: Special Child Publications.

Silver, R. (1991). *Stimulus drawings and techniques in therapy, development, and assessment.* Sarasota, Florida: Ablin Press Distributors.

Silver, R. 1992. Gender differences in drawings: a study of self-images, autonomous subjects, and relationships. *Art Therapy: Journal of the American Art Therapy Association, 9*(2), 85–92.

Silver, R. (1993a). *Draw a Story: Screening for depression and age or gender differences.* Sarasota, Florida, Ablin Press Distributors.

Silver, R. (1993b). Age and gender differences expressed through drawings: A study of attitudes toward self and others. *Art Therapy, 10*(3), 159–168. ERIC EJ 502 654

Silver, R. (1993c). Assessing the emotional content of drawings by older adults, *Art Therapy: American Journal of Art Therapy, 32,* 46–52.

Silver, R. (1996a). *Silver Drawing Test of cognition and emotion.* Sarasota, Florida: Ablin Press Distributors.

Silver, R. (1996b). Sex differences in the solitary and assaultive fantasies of delinquent and nondelinquent adolescents. *Adolescence, 31*(123), 543–552. ERIC EJ # 535 383

Silver, R. (1996c). Gender differences and similarities in the spatial abilities of adolescents. *Art Therapy: Journal of the American Art Therapy Association, 13*(2), 118–120. ERIC EJ 530 390.

Silver, R. (1997). Sex and age differences in attitides toward the opposite sex. *Art Therapy: Journal of the American Art Therapy Association, 14*(4), 268–272.

Silver, R. (1998a). Gender parity and disparity in spatial skills: Comparing horizontal, vertical, and other task performances. *Art Therapy: Journal of the American Art Therapy Association, 15*(1), 38–46.

Silver, R. (1998b). *Updating the SDT & DAS Manuals.* New York: Ablin Press.

Silver, R. (1999a). *Studies in art therapy, 1962–1998.* Sarasota, FL: Ablin Press Distributors.

Silver, R. (1999b). Differences among aging and young adults in attitudes and cognition. *ARTherapy, Journal of the American Art Therapy Association,*

Silver, R. (2000a). *Studies in art therapy, 1962–1998.* Sarasota, FL: Ablin Press Distributors.

Silver, R. (2000b). *Developing cognitive and creative skills through art: Programs for children with communication disorders.* Baltimore: University Park Press. Author' Guild Backinprint.com Edition. iuniverse.com. ERIC ED # 410 479 209 878.

Silver, R. (2000c). Silver Drawing Test Supplement. Sarasota, Florida: Ablin Press Distributors.

Silver, R. & Carrion, F. (1991). Using the Silver Drawing Test in school and hospital. *American Jourrnal of Art Therapy, 30*(2), 36–43.

Silver R. & Ellison, J. (1995). Identifying and assessing self-images in drawings by delinquent adolescents. *The Arts in Psychotherapy, 22*(4), 339–352. ERIC EJ 545 763

Silver, R. & Lavin, C. (1977). The role of art in developing and evaluating cognitive skills, *Journal of Learning Disabilities, 10*(7), 416–424. ERIC ED # 101 654, EJ # 171 839.

Silver, R., Lavin, C., Boeve, E., Hayes, K., Itzler, J., O'Brien, J., Terner, N., & Wohlberg, P. (1980). *Assessing and developing cognitive skills in handicapped children through art.* National Institution of Education Project # G 79 0081. New York: College of New Rochelle. ERIC ED #209878.

Sinclair-deZwart, H. (1969). Developmental Psycholinguistics. In D. Ellcind (Ed.) Studies in Cognitive Development. Oxford Press: London.

Sless, D. S. (1981). *Learning and visual communication.* New York: John Wiley & Sons.

Smith, M. D. et al. (1977). Intellectual characteristics of school labeled learning disabled children. *Exceptional Child, 4*(6), 352–357.

Sonstroem, A. M. (1966). On the conservatuion of solids. In J. S. Bruner et al., op cit.

SRA Reading achievement test and SRA Survey of Basic Skills Ability, 1978–1987. McMillan-McGraw Hill, CA: Montery.

Tannen, D. (1990). *You just don't understand.* New York: Ballantine Books.

Tinnen, L. (1990). Biological processes in nonverbal commincation and their role in the making and interpretation of art. *American Journal of Art Therapy, 29,* 9–13.

Thomas, H., Janison, W., and Hammer, D. (1973). Observation is insufficient for discovering that the surface of still water is invariantly horizontal. *Science, 181,* p. 173.

Torrance, E. P. (1980). Creative intelligence and an agenda for the 80s. *Art Education, 33*(7), 8–14.

Torrance, E. P. (1984). *The Torrance Test of Creative Thinking, Figural Form A*. Bensonville, IL: Scholastic Testing Service.

Ulman, E. (1987). *Ulman Personality Assessment Procedure*. Montpelier, Vermont: American Journal of Art Therapy.

Turner, C. (1993). The Draw a Story in assessment of abuse. Preconference Course Presentation at the 1993 Conference of the American Art Therapy Association, Atlanta, GA.

WAIS (Wechsler Adult Intelligence Scale, 1971–1991. Psychological Corp., TX: San Antonio.

Wilson, M. F. (1990). *Art therapy as an adjunctive treatment modality with depressed hospitalized adolescents*. Unpublished master's thesis, Ursuline College, Pepper Pike, Ohio. University Microfilms #5420.

Wilson, M. F. (1993). Assessment of brain Injury patients with the Draw a Story Instrument. Preconference Course Presentation at the 1993 Conference of the American Art Therapy Association, Atlanta, Georgia, Nov. 18–22 1993.

Winer, B. W. (1962). *Statistical principles in experimental design*. New York: McGraw-Hill.

Witkin, H. A., Dyk, R. B., Faterson, H. F., Goodenough, D. R., and Karp, S. A. (1962). *Psychological differentiation*. New York: John Wiley & Sons.

WSIC (Wechsler Intelligence Scale for Children), 1971–1991. Psychological Corp., TX: San Antonio.

Ziv, A. (1984). *Personality and sense of humor*. New York: Springer Publishing.

INDEX